Hail Babylon!

ALSO BY ANDREI CODRESCU

MEMOIRS
Road Scholar
The Hole in the Flag: An Exile's Story of Return and Revolution
In America's Shoes
The Life and Times of an Involuntary Genius

NONFICTION
Ay, Cuba!
The Dog with the Chip in His Neck
Zombification
The Muse Is Always Half-Dressed in New Orleans
The Disappearance of the Outside
Raised by Puppets Only to Be Killed by Research
A Craving for Swan

POETRY
Belligerence
Comrade Past and Mister Present
Selected Poems: 1970-1980
Diapers on the Snow
Necrocorrida
For the Love of a Coat
The Lady Painter
The Marriage of Insult and Injury
A Mote Suite for Jan and Anselm
Grammar and Money
A Serious Morning
Secret Training
the, here, what, where
The History of the Growth of Heaven
License to Carry a Gun

FICTION
Messiah
The Blood Countess
Monsieur Teste in America and Other Instances of Realism
The Repentance of Lorraine
Why Can't I Talk on the Telephone

Andrei Codrescu

PICADOR USA

NEW YORK

Hail Babylon!

NPR'S ROAD SCHOLAR GOES IN SEARCH OF THE AMERICAN CITY

Picador® is a U.S. registered trademark and is used by St. Martin's Press under license from Pan Books Limited.

For information on Picador USA Reading Group Guides, as well as ordering, please contact the Trade Marketing department at St. Martin's Press.
Phone: 1-800-221-7945 extension 763
Fax: 212-677-7456
E-mail: trademarketing@stmartins.com

Design by Maureen Troy

Library of Congress Cataloging-in-Publication Data

Codrescu, Andrei.
    Hail Babylon! : NPR's road scholar goes in search of the American city /
by Andrei Codrescu.
        p.   cm.
    Includes bibliographical references.
    ISBN 0-312-18107-8 (hc)
    ISBN 0-312-20653-4 (pbk)
    1. United States—Description and travel.   2. Cities and towns—
United States.   3. Codrescu, Andrei, 1946– —Journeys—United
States.   4. United States—Social conditions—1980–   I. Title.
E169.04.C644   1998
973.92—dc21
                                                                    97-36466
                                                                    CIP

First Picador USA Paperback Edition: June 1999

10 9 8 7 6 5 4 3 2 1

To my friends, citizens all

CONTENTS

Contents

INTRODUCTION

The gist of histories and statistics as far back as the records reach is
  in you this hour, and myths and tales the same,
If you were not breathing and walking here, where would they all be?
The most renown'd poems would be ashes, orations and plays would
  be vacuums.

All architecture is what you do to it when you look upon it,
(Did you think it was the white or gray stone? or the lines of the
  arches and cornices?)

—Walt Whitman, "A Song for Occupations"

When cities were first founded, an old Egyptian scribe tells us, the mission of the founder was to "put the gods in their places." The task of the coming city is not essentially different: its mission is to put the highest concerns of man at the center of all his activities: to unite the scattered fragments of the human personality, turning artificially dismembered men—bureaucrats, specialists, "experts," depersonalized agents—into complete human beings, repairing the damage that has been done by vocational separation, by the overcultivation of a favored function, by tribalisms and nationalisms, by the absence of organic partnerships and ideal purposes.

—Lewis Mumford, *The City in History*

Being human is itself difficult, and therefore all kinds of settlements (except dream cities) have problems. Big cities have difficulties in abundance, because they have people in abundance. But vital cities are not helpless to combat even the most difficult of problems. They are not passive victims of chains of circumstances, any more than they are the malignant opposite of nature.

—Jane Jacobs, "The Death and Life of Great American Cities"

The three philosophers of the city quoted above are all Americans and proud of their American cities. Walt Whitman, who hadn't yet seen the abominations of suburbs, exurbs, gated communities, public housing projects, and cyclone-fenced high-rises, praised the city for its energy, multifariousness, and openness. His city was New York, to which he referred by its Indian name, Manahatta; she filled him with the poetry of her streets, the sexiness of her throngs, and her dream-inducing waterfront. Whitman would have been outraged by a sexless, empty collection of guarded, standoffish buildings that shut down at night after swallowing their residents directly from shapeless tin cans in hideous underground garages. He would have been equally appalled by vast manicured lawns leading up to castle-sized buildings from which only the sound of televisions could be heard. The city for Whitman was that meeting place where humans inspired by each other's proximity invented themselves and their institutions while swimming strongly *with* the mighty currents of industry and commerce. Whitman's city righted itself by constant movement, weaknesses and strengths always finding new balance within the ebb and flow of the streets.

Lewis Mumford, in his sprawling polemic, *The City in History*, views the organism of the city with a less poetic, though no less sympathetic, eye. The job of making better human beings falls to the "ideal city," the blueprints for which lie buried in the imperfect mess we inhabit today. "Putting the gods in their place" is the operation of a united, willful community.

Creating a competitive reality, whether meant to awaken the gods, or to overthrow them, has been the ambition of every utopian enterprise. The latest of these, "virtual reality," aims, precisely, to be reality's competitor, its alternative and, eventually, its undoing. The seduction of utopian rhetoric is undeniable; it is kept in check only by the miserable evidence of trying to implement it. Unfortunately, evidence is no deterrent. Even today, Platonism dominates what is called city planning, which proceeds blindly out of the Platonic vision into utopian translation, without stopping on the way for anything like flesh-and-blood human beings.

Jane Jacobs's famous essay, "The Death and Life of Great American Cities," is a cri de coeur against the Plato-utopic beast. Cities, she argues, are where human beings, those complex, paradoxical creatures live; they make a world according to their measure, not the plans of utopia-sick bureaucrats. Jacobs describes the successes and failures of cities at the level of everyday interactions, moods of the streets, exchanges in public spaces, and the spontaneous organizations of the socius.

I am a city boy from way back. I was born in Romania in the medieval burg of Sibiu—Hermanstadt in German, Nagyszebenbe in Hungarian—founded around the year 900. Legend has it that the Pied Piper of Hamlin piped the children of Germany over the mountains and brought them here. Sibiu sits on a plateau surrounded by the Carpathian Mountains and is walled on all sides in readiness for whatever might come at it from any direction. Whatever *did* come at it from every direction. Founded by wealthy German merchants, the city was ripe for plunder: sacking and burning it was a sport throughout the Middle Ages. Vlad Dracula, the real man behind the Dracula legend, plundered Sibiu, then impaled most of its prominent citizens in the town square. He ordered banquet tables set up and invited the remaining burghers to feast among the agony cries of their neighbors. When his table companions complained, Dracula had them impaled on higher stakes so they wouldn't hear the screaming.

This was the way to sack a city. The only thing that came close in my lifetime was when the Hell's Angels took their vacation in Monte Rio, California, a small town I lived in for a time in the mid-seventies. The Angels burned down a couple of buildings, shot a couple of natives, and terrorized the rest of us. We spent an anxious weekend behind doors, with shotguns, while the sheriff called in reinforcements from Santa Rosa.

The city square in Sibiu, where Dracula stuck our better citizens, was also used for burning witches in the late sixteenth century. This time the danger did not come from the outside to breach the city walls, but from the inside. For this, there is no equivalent in my experience, though my current residence, New Orleans, is no stranger to irate mobs rising against each other for similarly occult reasons.

In the seventeenth century, Baron von Bruckenthal, the governor of Transylvania, and the lover of the Austrian empress Maria Theresa, began filling his palace on the square with paintings his lover "borrowed" from the Vienna gallery. In addition to being a lover of art, the baron was also an inventor. He invented instruments of torture, notably the rack wheel, used to crush a particularly irksome rebel.

In 1947, one year after I was born, Baron von Bruckenthal's palace became the headquarters of the Communist Party, the new ruler of

Romania. The square became the site of May Day demonstrations and other public festivities where the population marched, waved banners, and shouted slogans for the Party brass standing on a platform.

In 1989, the Communist regime fell and I returned to Sibiu. The town square had been the site of a huge demonstration against the Communists, and a battlefield. An improvised shrine to people killed there by secret police snipers was leaning against the statue of the nineteenth-century educator, Gheorghe Lazar, surrounded by flowers and burning candles.

My medieval town square was the center of the city. All civic life, since the founding, revolved around the city center. This is true of all European cities. You can imagine my disappointment in Detroit, in 1966, when, as a freshly arrived immigrant, I walked for miles past the hulks of burnt-out factories and shabby neighborhoods (although most of the houses were bigger than those in Sibiu) and was unable to find the center. When I arrived, around seven P.M. in an area called "downtown," the place was deserted.

American cities are new, have no walls, fear no outside enemies, and their public squares (Salem excepted) have seen no witch burnings. Their founding myths are tenuous. They were not founded by wolf-suckling twins like Romulus and Remus, or Daedalus, who lay down the blueprints and vanished. The founders of cities called New York, New Haven, New Orleans, New Brunswick, et cetera, relied on the word "new" to evoke the old, but "new" is only a skeuomorph, a meaning-empty appellation that establishes a merely formal connection with the past. In fact, New York is nothing like York, and New Orleans is certainly no Orléans. The cities of the New World were carved out by industry and given character by men like Henry Siegel and Frank Cooper (who built New York's Siegel-Cooper store), John Wanamaker of Philadelphia, Jordan Marsh of Boston. The cathedrals of the new world were called Macy's, Marshall Field's, and Hudson's. If the cities of the East Coast looked back at Europe for their nominal historic continuity, the cities of the West looked back to the East, which for them was already the "old world." Portland, Oregon, for instance, was named by a Portland, Maine, businessman who won a coin toss with a man from Boston, Massachusetts. The city could have just as easily been called Boston. With the exception of Salt Lake City, no American city can claim to have been founded by divine revelation. But the barons of industry were gods in their own right who deployed brash new styles for their new cities. The upward thrust of American optimism pierced the skies as surely as the spires of European Gothic cathedrals, with little fear about what sky gods they might be displacing. Night was banished by waves of electricity; bright signage and enormous displays created an entirely different sky, such as the old world had never known. The startling newness of the American urban sky, evident to newcomers, was captured by Walker Evans in his photographs of signs; he captured the new language of twentieth-century America.

There is no telling where American cities might have gone at the end of the nineteenth and beginning of the twentieth centuries if the lords of industry had gone on untaxed and unabashed. The Tribune Tower Building in Chicago might give a clue: imbedded in its side are large chunks of rock from famous places in the world: the Great Wall of China, the Great Pyramid at Giza, the Pyramid of the Sun at Teotihuacán, and so on. Wealthy American tourists in the early days of the century must have thought nothing was amiss with carting off large chunks of other peoples' sacred sites. Gone unchecked, this penchant for magnitude might have carted the monuments of the whole world back to America; instead of a London Bridge here and there, we might be traipsing through Notre-Dame and the Alhambra in St. Louis and Denver. (Converted to multiuse, of course, especially shopping.)

Today, such arrogance is inconceivable. Taxes and the anger of the hoi polloi (both domestic and foreign) took the wind out of some of the more ostentatious capitalists. After the Great Depression, personal wealth became discreet. Corporate wealth did not, but the corporate style, no matter the renown of its architects, had nothing seductive about it. Towers built since the midcentury are impersonal, self-contained worlds that crushed whole neighborhoods, and dwarfed what they didn't crush. Many of these megabuildings look like ruins already, cities of the dead meant to be unearthed by archaeologists. In the 1970s, the fear of "terrorists" gave birth to monstrous, windowless fortresses in the style commonly known as Nixon-Mitchell architecture. These buildings are so unfriendly—the Federal Building in Baltimore is a prime example—that anyone entering them feels like a criminal. These buildings suppress democratic, civic life as much as the pyramids looming over the toiling Aztecs.

The damage inflicted on cities by corporate megabuildings was matched only by the damage wrought by federal building projects. In the 1960s, an orgy of demolition for highways destroyed the soul of more than one great American city. Happily, here and there, in cities like New Orleans, corruption and laziness prevented the big money from destroying *everything*. In some lucky spots, the scale shrank instead of bloating, and more than one variety of blessed decay kept some cities human. Happily too, the automobile exodus to the suburbs sapped the tax base of some old cities, leaving them to languish until the nineties when, *grazie a Dio*, a different thinking started putting out tender shoots.

But we are hardly out of the woods yet. To halt "the decay" (a notion with many definitions), most American cities, big and small, have city planning offices now, staffed by city planners. These secular servants of the city are rarely philosophers of the city, though their provenance can be easily traced to the Plato-utopic urges described by Lewis Mumford. Many medium-sized and small American cities' planning offices are really "surrender offices," in the job of handing their cities over to the first enemies that demand their surrender. Strip malls driven by huge Wal-Marts arrive outside the city limits just as Dracula once did. But where the old Transylvanian cities put up a valiant defense, modern American cities just surrender. In exchange, they don't get sacked or burned to the ground right away; they wither over time, as their populations gravitate to the Great Sprawl outside their centers.

American cities have political enemies, too. Take Speaker Newt Gingrich's proposal to endow every welfare recipient with a laptop computer. The immediate effect would be to disperse the poor, just like the affluent. If you can work from anywhere, you don't need to be in a city. The virtual communities of the future will be the very opposite of cities. Instead of living in a sensual world, people will be connected by mental effort. The abandonment of the cities would certainly benefit the political class most afraid of what the cities contain: blacks, Jews, Latinos, Asians, other ethnics, homosexuals, bohemians, artists.

The best features of the American cities I have seen are quite often their mixed neighborhoods, the places where the greatest and most diverse number of people live, areas where there are a lot of bars and restaurants, catering to both the people who live above or behind them, and sad tourists looking for life. Most American tourists are sad, because they come from lifeless suburbs, dead-end roads, private and deserted developments. When they get to North Beach in San Francisco, to the French Quarter in New Orleans, to Greenwich Village in New York, to Fells Point in Baltimore, or to any number of preserved, rescued, or re-created old neighborhoods, they experience something akin to pleasure. A well-furnished tourist trap can cause bliss in an amnesiac or, anyway, someone without the memory of a real city, someone without an *organ* for the urban pleasures.

I believe that we are now at a crossroads in America. The dying city is being rethought, but it is still being attacked and destroyed, (though at a slower pace). Clearly, we cannot afford to lose the cultural and social engines of the great cities. Efforts are being made to reclaim them. Many people who have experienced the Great Sprawl are returning to the cities. Those who never gave up on them, either because they were too poor, or too stubborn, are finding themselves wooed. The new thinking is reclaiming neighborhoods, rediscovering history, and rebuilding public transportation. The old thinking is still razing neighborhoods, putting up towers, and throwing up freeways through the heart of communities. Myriad tensions attend the conflict.

What follows is a collection of observations about cities big and small, made sometimes at leisure, sometimes on the run. While most of the essays are about particular cities, some are intended to intuit the spirit of a region, and of the people who inhabit it. Quite often what's *around* a city, especially great scenic beauty, can say much about the mind and the future of it. Little Rock, Arkansas, would be meaningless without the Ozark country of Arkansas. At times, I let myself reflect on other aspects of a city's aura, for instance, the notion of the South and what it means being Southern. The South is preponderant, because this is where I live.

The cities presented herein are in a kind of backwards order, proceeding outward from the South. I like to think that this arrangement is not purely idiosyncratic, but based on something I call Time Reservoirs. The city of New Orleans and the region of the South seem to me to contain more time in their Time Reservoirs than the cities of the West, which contain more than the cities of the North. I begin in New Orleans, to me the most timeless city, and end in New York, the most seemingly timebound. Both cities skeuomorph on New and both claim time in their newspapers: the *New Orleans Times-Picayune* and the *New York Times*. Between New Orleans and New York stretches the fifteen hundred miles of frontline in America's meanest war: that between time and timelessness.

The timelessness of New Orleans, enforced by the cotton softness of the dream-imbued and nightmare-rattled region of the South, is deeply haunted by the urgency of time in the guise of economic development and tourism over a background of corrupt politics and crime. New York, on the other hand, chopped to pieces as it is by the guillotine hands of global-economy time, hides pockets of timelessness yet, possible precisely because so much stays behind while the race speeds on.

What I have hunted, in my duties as soldier and spy, within the cities of these United States is precisely the presence of timelessness, represented by stubborn pockets of resistance within our urban scapes. On the other hand, my travels were only the product of chance assignments. That any order is discernible may only be my fancy. When I was six years old a Gypsy woman folded me in her voluminous skirts and read my palm. "You will travel far," was all she was able to say before my irate mother snatched me off her lap, and shooed her away. I like to think that she might have added, ". . . and it will all make sense." Maybe. You tell me.

PART ONE

CLARENCE LAUGHLIN: *The End of an Era*
(COURTESY OF THE PHOTOGRAPHER)

New Orleans

My nature is the city. Not any city: only those cities, like New Orleans, which have become nature. Here, there are doors older than most American trees, street corners dense with the psychic substance of past events, manhole covers that can be read just like a natural formation. This kind of city accrues a nature to itself over time: doors *are* trees, street corners are hot springs, manhole covers are arroyos. Forms become organic through use: who can deny that jazz can have the force of wind, or that café au lait at Kaldi's on a rainy day is possessed of duration?

I am arguing, I guess, against the hackneyed opposition between nature and civilization, with its residues of guilt and recrimination. Sure, at some point doors replaced trees, but that was a (relatively) long time ago. Long enough, anyway, for weeds to crack through the cobblestones, and for flowers, vines, grass, live oaks, palms, figs, and banana trees to grow and disappear. Long enough for the resident life forms to reach a modus vivendi, to change and die and be remembered and forgotten. The peculiar thing about human nature is its ability to regret its past, when nature was more natural. And cities are the centers, par excellence, of this regret. I doubt very much if human beings bereft of this city-born nostalgia could even have a feeling for nature. I'm not talking about ideology (that human thing) here but about sentiment (that natural thang). Both nature and civilization are metaphors. It cannot be otherwise: we can only understand where we live through how we feel about it. If we love it and it makes us feel good, it's nature. Otherwise, it's the state, or civilization.

New Orleans is a creature of the river, much as Egypt (before the Aswan Dam) used to be a creature of the Nile. Nestled in the crook of the river, the crescent-shaped city does not follow the cardinal points. The Mississippi River is the only reference: away or toward the river, downriver or upriver. At night, when you can't sleep because the above paradox keeps you awake, you hear the whistles and horns of barges and the churning of the river. When it's foggy, they get so loud they wake up the birds who respond with piercing cries. And then you have to get up, and you see that the moon is full too, and the smell of river mud has barged in, thick and sensuous. And you put on the honey-silk voice of Aaron Neville who tells you that "it feels like rain." And you can be sure that it does, and that if someone is there, next to you, you'll be making love. And if no one is, you'll be immersed in that no-name regret, that bottomless longing for that nameless something. And if this isn't nature, then what can it be?

Nor does this feeling recede the next morning when you walk the full three miles from your gardenia-smothered lair to Cafe du Monde for beignets and café au lait. The dawn has broken over the river. Both sides are gold: the steamboats and foreign ships on your side, and the West Bank on the opposite shore. The ships are floating above your head because you are *under* the river, a surreal perspective that never becomes routine. New Orleans is a bowl surrounded by levees: if they break, the bowl fills up and that's the end of us. Like Venice, Italy, this is a place of fleeting beauty. The knowledge that we won't be here long gives everyone an intense appetite for living. Or just an appetite:

today, at Mike's on the Avenue, the special is barbequed oysters with ginger and pancetta. Recommended.

Someone living in the Louisiana bayous, in the Atchafalaya Basin, let's say, might meditate daily on the fragility of this river-built world. While pulling up his crab trap or digging for crawfish, he might wonder what he is doing in the annihilating heat of the day, prey to legions of insects and snakes twisted like spaghetti, when he could be in the cool mountains, lying flat on a boulder, surveying the valley below. I think of that someone while I eat his superbly prepared catch and wonder what *I* am doing here, in a city of decay, crime, filth, and stench, when I could be in, let's say, Jerusalem, a city of ideas and stone.

New Orleans is in many ways the opposite of Jerusalem. It is most definitely not a holy city. The only religion that lays claim to the streets of the Vieux Carré is that ruled by Carnival, a cult of sensuousness, sin, unconsciousness, dreams, masques, shifting identities, exaltation of the flesh. New Orleans is all flesh, Jerusalem is all spirit. This flesh of ours makes sounds, deep and mournful, or orgiastic and rapturous, sounds that are prearticulate and too rich to be articulate. Jerusalem, on the other hand, laments and articulates, quarrels and specifies, laments and records. New Orleans is the slow-flowing mud of soul, Jerusalem, the hard stones of spirit. But one thing these cities have in common: they are both cemeteries. New Orleans, not nearly as old as Jerusalem, is yet a collection of graves surrounding the living. At St. Louis No. 1, for instance, you stand before the eroded angel and the iron cross at the grave of Monsieur Robert Armant, a Creole already dead in the last century, and wonder what relation if any he had to Camille Tainturier, her stone-flowers relief almost touching his. You put down your coffee on a broken urn and sit on his cracked stone, next to a wreath of plastic blue roses. Monsieur Robert was no Jesus, he founded no religion, but something about his dwelling place makes you think that he was a swashbuckling knight and a charming persuader, no less. Or maybe it's all wishful thinking: the nature of my mind.

The air is only slightly thinner than the rich mud the city is planted in. Geologists call this soil *gumbo*, because just like the brown roux thickened for hours over a low flame, it is slow and unsteady, its only job to trap flavors and to return them. We can't bury our dead in it because the corpses would float out into the streets so we build above-ground tombs that look like bread ovens. New Orleans cemeteries look like vast bakeries quietly holding the ancestral loaves. This is no idle metaphor in a city that loves its dead as much as its food. The sense that life and death are locked in amorous gourmandise is everywhere.

From the upstairs picture window at Commander's Palace, one of my favorite eateries, one can glimpse the Lafayette Cemetery through the branches of a huge live oak. Nobody, as far as I know, has written a comprehensive guide to the fine restaurants that line the edges of New Orleans cemeteries, but it would be worth a try. How much subtler the texture of lightly fried oysters, the smoky sexiness of a dark roux, the vibrant redness of alligator piquant in the light of our mortality! This is perhaps what gives any old restaurant in New Orleans its deeply felt sense of hedonism and melancholy. And if a jazz funeral is being held, perhaps the procession might stop in for free drinks. It is customary for the mourners, led by the musician friends of the departed, to pause en route in places where the deceased had libations.

The nature of New Orleans is to encourage the optimum development of New Orleanians: it's an environment for a specific life form, a dreamy, lazy, sentimental, musical one, prey to hallucinations (not visions), tolerant, indolent, and gifted at storytelling. This goes against the very grain of American civilization as we know it. We lie incongruously in the way of the thrifty, Puritan America whose concerns, including environmental ones, are driven by the logic of economies and planning. We, and our ways, are marked for elimination; there is no room in an efficient future for what we embody. Like the moon we ought to be blown up, for interfering with the weather. This is a city of night, fog, and mud, the three elements against which all the might of America is mobilized.

The nature of New Orleans, I propose, is no less endangered than the nature of the Amazon. If the Amazon be protected—and I pray it is—then we ought to receive the same care too. Our indefinable layering of sounds and sentimentalities should be defended against the endless suburbs spreading like mosquito clouds out of the swamps to the East. It should be, but by whom? Not, I hope, by the gratingly articulate bureaucrats of heritage. Nor by those who would expand the metaphor of nature to take in cities. By whom then? By no one. If we are doomed—by the river or by something else—then so be it. This is how nature becomes natural.

Tourists experience New Orleans by guidebook geography, which recognizes only three areas: the French Quarter, the Garden District, and Audubon Park. Those distinctions ignore the many other neighborhoods—Faubourg Marigny, Irish Channel, Ninth Ward, Garden District, Uptown, Carrollton—to mention only a few. Each of these minifiefdoms is culturally distinct, a laboratory for the color palette of New Orleans, which mixes black, Indian, Creole, and white. The intricate relations of these cultures to one another can be seen all at once at Mardi Gras. At that time, the city tells its story in music and masks. It's not a simple or sentimental story: it's a gritty, often painful tale of clashing cultures and races that miraculously transcend themselves for the orgiastic space of a few days.

The first summer I spent here, in 1985, I was sure that my brains were boiling, and if it weren't for the cool barrooms where I scribbled nonsense on napkins, I would have surely evaporated. I read several educational books about the place, including the Creole romances of

George Washington Cable, Lafcadio Hearn's minigothics, a charming and scary book called *The French Quarter* by Herbert Asbury, and, finally, *A Confederacy of Dunces*, by John Kennedy Toole. I was bowled over by Toole: I laughed the way I laughed when I first read *Don Quixote*, *The Good Soldier Schweik*, and *Dead Souls*. These were big-time HaHas of Great Comedy, not chuckles of polite empathy. On the Scale of Mirth, which I have devised, The Big HaHas are Top Dogs, filled with godlike indifference to the reader's cherished opinions.

My friend Philip Herter, who'd given it to me, told me that this was *the* New Orleans book. Philip, whom I first met in Mexico, had also told me that Malcolm Lowry's *Under the Volcano* was the book to read in Mexico and he was right. I hoped however that *A Confederacy* would be gentler on my body than *Volcano* had been: in honor of Lowry I'd tried to replicate the consul's journey through the mezcal bars and ended up alcohol poisoned for a week.

Well, there was no such danger in *A Confederacy*, at least not such an obvious and immediate one. There was nothing and nobody in it worthy of emulating. Everyone was a pathos-filled victim whose existence was rigorously predicated on a no-exit stupidity from which no faith or superstition would ever free them. Ignatius J. Reilly, a late-fifties, early-sixties Don Quixote, tilted at the windmills of a provincial world barely shaken by the gale-force winds loose in the rest of America. Like Don Quixote, Ignatius was a one-man compendium of shabbiness fighting an imaginary future with equally imaginary values. His presence guaranteed disaster and yet no one emerged unchanged from the encounter. In fact, Ignatius's disastrous interventions improved everyone's situation in the end. I closed the book with unbounded admiration for the author, an admiration doubled by regret. Toole committed suicide after being unable to persuade anyone to publish his masterpiece.

My admiration wasn't strictly for the book but also for the city that permitted the writing of such a book. Its existence belied, paradoxically, the setting of the book itself. As a newcomer I felt that this was indeed a blessed place, capable of unabashedly advertising its flaws, fearing no ridicule and no criticism. That, in essence, is the opposite of provincialism. The great cities of the world are not provincial: they invite complexity, not propaganda. New York, Venice, Paris, or Prague exist in literature as exemplary occasions for meditation. They invite bitterness as well as joy, comedy as much as indictment. Additionally, they continue to exist outside their literature like great beasts or great beauties who become more themselves the more they are photographed, loved, or whipped.

Provincialism, on the other hand, is the exact opposite. The terror of being badly spoken of outweighs all distinctions. Places are affected by degrees of provincialism that can get better or worse. In the seventies, Washington, D.C., for instance, had a provincial envy of New York, as did Chicago to some extent. I don't think Chicago does any longer, but I'm not so sure about Washington. Baltimore and Little Rock have no such problems because it would never occur to anyone to compare their cultures with that of the capitals. San Francisco had and has a huge streak of insecurity vis-à-vis almost any place the same size or bigger. Size, as some girls say, has nothing to do with it. My own hometown of Sibiu in Transylvania, Romania, boasts a body of literature much greater than its modest dimensions. Genius incubates within a peculiar pride of place, created partly by unapologetic quirkiness, and partly by a quixotic detachment from facts. I was sure that New Orleans was just such a place on the evidence of Ignatius J. Reilly.

The question of the book's rejection was interesting. A *Confederacy of Dunces* was a book that swam upstream, away from the flow of the time when it was written. The early sixties saw the awakening of a social conscience that even the great postwar comic novels, *Catch-22*,

Cat's Cradle, and *Portnoy's Complaint*, were part of. Their charges were delivered pretty squarely from behind the barricades of antiestablishment liberalism. The incipient tentacles of what came to be known in the nineties as political correctness were already waving within the embryonic culture of the sixties. The South, at the beginning of the civil rights movement, was America's designated Hell. Southern writers were a suspect species with a few rare exceptions, including Walker Percy, who eventually, after Toole died, championed the book into print. *A Confederacy's* unabashed use of Negro dialect by Jones, the floor sweeper, and the fun-poking at the spirit-filled black factory workers must have repulsed New York publishers, if they had read the book at all, which is doubtful. There was also the matter of a slew of prancing queens, an evil madam, and a bumbling cop who was a victim, not a villain. And then there was Myrna Minx, the Jewish firebrand sexual revolutionary whose sheer silliness was matched only by Ignatius's megalomania. It was as if Toole had set out deliberately to turn the stereotypes on their heads, which is, of course, precisely what he did. The failure of American publishers to see this is pretty unforgivable and proof, more than anything, of a New York brand of provincialism. I am not sure if John Kennedy Toole's suicide was a direct result of his rejection, but even if this played only a small part, the fools have a lot to answer for. Toole's job was far from done.

Thirteen years have passed since my first reading of *A Confederacy of Dunces*. My exalted view of New Orleans as a gloriously unprovincial city has taken a skeptical turn. The city, as represented by its cultural establishment, is a mess of uneasy contradictions. On the one hand, it declares its sicknesses poetic, on the other it denies them. In proof of the poetry, the city trots out the considerable artistic products of some of its past and current citizens, including Toole's masterwork. In denial, it reduces whatever bitter diagnoses those works reveal to an even paste of booster pride, suitable for feeding tourists. Great books were written here, the city says, but please don't read them. I get so *embarrassed*. If one recognizes Blanche in that feint, one is not wrong. New Orleans *is* Blanche Dubois, and that mix of knowledge, denial, hunger, and experience is precisely what makes her so attractive to outsiders. Those who are not outsiders and who know her only too well have mixed feelings. And what is an outsider anyway? I was told that if your *grand-mere* didn't go to school here you're an outsider. And school means Catholic grade school. For practical purposes, I would say that ten years about suffices to become, if not an insider, then at least a familiar.

My familiarity with the city enables me to offer another reading of this book now. *A Confederacy of Dunces* is the work of an insider, a genuine act of treason by someone with access to all the privileged information. Toole was a traitor and no amount of rehabilitative boosterism can erase the stigma. To this day, people tiptoe around the content of *A Confederacy of Dunces* for myriad reasons, chief among them being that the mirror this book holds up makes the natives wince. Typical in this regard was the response of my undergraduate class, which contained a number of older students from New Orleans.

More than half of them said that they didn't like *A Confederacy of Dunces*. Didn't you laugh? I asked them. Not really. Some of those who couldn't even manage a chuckle were intimately familiar with the milieu of the novel. One woman, who had been born right on Constantinople Street, where Ignatius J. Reilly lived with his mother, said that she was personally offended by the intimate squalor of the characters. They were caricatures, she said.

Nothing could be further from the truth. The characters of John Kennedy Toole's novel are the very opposite of caricatures: they are ultra-realist depictions of a time and place, complete with nose hairs, cataracts, swollen feet, warts, intestinal distress, political opinions, and social codes. Ignatius Reilly, the gargantuan slob who torments everyone with his artistic genius, is a merciless camera lens trained on an eternal stupidity that, far from dated, flourishes unchecked in our day.

The dislike of Reilly's neighbor is easy to understand. It's the same dislike that caused the parents of my friend Michael Stephens to stop talking to him after he published his family saga, *Season at Coole*. My own mother was more than upset by my autobiographical novel, *The Life & Times of an Involuntary Genius*. A writer hurts the ones he loves because he knows them. This is basic stuff.

Another student found the novel offensive for its depictions of homosexuals, blacks, and women. Clearly, *A Confederacy of Dunces*, with its portraits of mincing queens, histrionic Negroes, and alcoholic women, could not be written today. It could have barely been written when Toole wrote it and it's a testimony to his genius that he did. It is also true that he treats these characters with a condescending tenderness that is lacking from his portraits of the bourgeois, people like Mr. and Mrs. Levy, the owners of Levy Pants, or Dr. Talc, the Tulane professor. This preferential treatment is the only concession that this otherwise equal-opportunity savager of a book makes to the time in which it was written.

Like Gogol's *Dead Souls*, *A Confederacy of Dunces* mirrors the profound provincialism of New Orleans in the early sixties. The city, where Ignatius rages at countless windmills, is a shabby backwater where everyone knows his place and suffers inordinately from the mild winds of change beginning to stir at the gates. The paranoia of the McCarthy era is still operative but is losing its bite. The old man who accuses everyone, including the police, of being "comuniss," is arrested. Jones, the floor sweeper at the Night of Joy Nightclub, is working on a strictly private plan for revenge. The workers at the Levy Pants factory, who are stirred by Ignatius's revolutionary fervor, have no idea what they are stirring for. The characters of the French Quarter have a great time playing games with the police. And the police, far from being agents of terror, are bumbling idiots.

Toole did not take on upper-crust New Orleans society and one can almost hear the sigh of relief. Think what he might have done with debutantes, Carnival kings and queens, oil-company execs, and today's art-fawning socialites. But the sigh is premature. Although Toole did not depict this layer of New Orleans directly, the book is still a mighty blow to the fantasy of the city that they like to maintain.

The last of my students to complain about the book said that it gave the city a bad image. With the aid of this observation, *A Confederacy of Dunces* comes full circle into utter relevance. Nostalgia is a full-time business in New Orleans, replete with manufactured glories, blessed by the chamber of commerce, and abetted by the cult of literary figures. John Kennedy Toole occupies an ambiguous place in this cult. He is lionized for his Pulitzer Prize–winning, posthumous accomplishment, but the content of his masterwork is still too raw for boosterism. Its uncomfortable truths still fly in the face of what everyone, from my students to cultural officialdom, would like to ignore. The book becomes more distressing as time goes by, an irony the young author might have appreciated.

A Confederacy of Dunces, though sometimes quoted, has never been intrinsically honored in New Orleans. There is nothing wrong with the annual fests of civic self-congratulation known as the Tennessee Williams Festival and the Faulkner Festival, but *A Confederacy of Dunces* Dunciad would be infinitely more appropriate, not to mention therapeutic.

I overheard a couple of young New Orleanians waxing lyrical about the time when "there weren't so many Americans in New Orleans. It was mostly Creole then." They remembered the summer mosquito swarms, when their mothers had to bundle them in raincoats with gloves on and scarves over their faces to take out the garbage. For all that, they still came back with mouths full of bugs. They remembered their parents remembering the yellow fever epidemics that carried off thousands. "They say things are rough now," one of them scoffed, "they were hell then."

It is easy to romanticize New Orleans—after all, dozens of writers, including Mark Twain, Walt Whitman, James Audubon, George Cable, and Lafcadio Hearn—did. They romanticized it down to its hideous summers, its muddy winters, its cutthroat streets, its gamblers, its crooked politicians, its whores. It was precisely from such corrupt gumbo that the dazzling flowers of its music—jazz, blues, Dixie—sprouted and dazzled the world. It was likewise with the telling and making of stories, the pageantry of Carnival, the complexity of dance, the subtleties of the palate. Hearing and admiring these *fleurs* the unwary tourist will sometime stumble into the living mud that feeds them.

Desuetude and pulchritude. Melancholy, exaltation, dejection. A naked man on a balcony. An ex-virgin still holding the plastic cup that held her first hurricane. A funeral wreath around a mule's neck. Two tired drag queens hiding from the light in a jasmine-choked portico. A flock of tuxedoed waiters streaming home before dawn. A troop of red ants feeding on dried beer on a rococo manhole. A voodoo shrine still smoking in the backyard. Smells of mud, perfume, chemicals. Cloying scent of something steamy and rotten wafting off a barge on the river. Another body found shot dead on the levee. Stories stacking up everywhere like coins in a street musician's sax case. Another New Orleans night is done.

But the night of March 4, 1995 was unusual even by our deviant standards. At one A.M. on March 4, 1995, policewoman Antoinette Frank ate supper at the Kim Anh restaurant, where she moonlighted as a guard. The two children of the Vietnamese family who owned the restaurant, Cuong Vu, seventeen, and Ha Vu, twenty-four, cooked her dinner. Frank's replacement, Officer Ronnie Williams, arrived to relieve her shift. About an hour later, Antoinette returned to the restaurant and knocked on the locked door. Officer Williams unlocked the door and let her in, thinking that she'd forgotten something. Frank was not alone. An eighteen-year-old named Roger Lacaze was with her.

Frank and Lacaze didn't waste any time. Ronnie Williams was killed with a bullet to the back of the head at short range and then two more shots were fired into him for insurance. The two children, who had stayed behind to clean up, begged for their lives. Cuong Vu was a junior in high school. He played football and was an altar boy at St. Brigid Church in eastern New Orleans. He wanted to be a priest. His sister wanted to be a nun. Frank told them to kneel and say their prayers. Cuong was pistol-whipped, then shot six times. His sister took three bullets.

Frank and Lacaze robbed the register and left the massacre scene. What happened afterward belongs to a different order of things. Antoinette Frank returned to the Seventh District police station, picked up a police car, and came back to the crime scene in uniform, in response to the 911 emergency call. Perhaps she wanted to make sure that no evidence was left behind. More likely, an insane bravado was at work. She believed that she had gotten away with murder. After all, other New Orleans policemen had. She had already gotten away with armed robbery, dealing drugs, and flaunting her ill-gotten goods. She had already given Lacaze, her partner in crime, a car, a beeper, and a cellular phone. At first, it was reported that Lacaze was her cousin, but later it was established that he was her love interest. Lacaze had a girlfriend who complained about Frank's attention, but was afraid to voice her complaints too loudly. Frank and Lacaze smoked and dealt crack and robbed people. In one perverse case, she arrested one of their complaining victims who was still in jail at the time of the Kim Anh massacre.

The crime scene was swarming with cops by the time she drove back. Among them was Richard Pennington, the new chief of police, who arrived as soon as he heard that a police officer had been shot. Antoinette, a petite, light-skinned black woman with a pleasing face, strode confidently into the blood-spattered scene and that's where her luck ended. Two of the murdered children's siblings had been hiding in a cooler in the restaurant and had witnessed everything. Quoc Vu, whose detailed testimony was key at the trial, heard her brother and sister's last prayers. She pointed out Frank as the killer. The policewoman was arrested on the spot.

Antoinette Frank was led from the Kim Anh restaurant by her fellow officers. She was smiling as she climbed into the backseat of a squad car. But this daring bandit and murderer was described by her fellow officers as "mousy." Indeed, there was nothing in Frank's records to indicate anything but an overwhelming mediocrity. She had failed the psychological evaluation required of prospective police officers. The psychiatrist who examined her said that she had a tendency to lie and an exaggerated sense of her own abilities, and he concluded that she should not be an officer. Frank was admitted to the police academy anyway, after she hired her own psychiatrist who gave her a better evaluation. Days before she became a police officer, she disappeared, leaving behind a note for her father. "I cannot live in this world the way I am," she wrote, and concluded, "I was doomed since the day I was born. I see that now. I hate myself and my life." Her father filed a missing person report. A few days later she returned and became a New Orleans police officer. Why was she hired? Two letters of recommendation, one from former New Orleans mayor Sidney Bartholomew, were repudiated by their writers. The ex-mayor claimed never to have signed the letter. But then, how was it possible for such an underqualified, would-be sociopath to join the ranks of the NOPD? Was there something rotten at the core of the system?

Antoinette Frank had an odd propensity to smile. "When she was supposed to be serious, like in self-defense stuff, she would be in there smiling and have to do push-ups constantly, because she couldn't take the smile off," an officer said. In her hometown of Opelousas, Louisiana, she was close to being completely unmemorable. Her English teacher said, "I don't even remember the girl, and it turns out she was in my homeroom." She even missed taking her yearbook picture. Her mother said, "She's something like me—she stayed mostly by herself." At the trial, her mother added, "Antoinette wouldn't hurt a fly."

In October 1995, Antoinette Frank became the first woman in Louisiana to receive the death penalty since 1940, when "Toni Jo" Henry was sentenced to death for killing a tire salesman in a rice field. Her accomplice, Roger Lacaze, was also condemned to death in a separate trial. But Antoinette Frank's saga was far from over.

A bizarre twist to the case occurred after she had already taken her place on death row. In September 1994 Frank had filed a missing person report on her father, Adam Frank, Sr. She was then living in eastern New Orleans. This, remember, was after her father had hired a missing person report on *her*. Her father, however, did not return. The new family now occupying the premises was unpleasantly surprised at dinner one night by their German shepherd that came in dragging a human bone. The bones found under Frank's former residence have not yet been identified.

The Kim Anh triple murder committed by an NOPD officer was the most spectacular case of the year, but it came after a long series of revelations of crimes committed by members of the department. The

SANDRA RUSSELL CLARK: *Cemetery*
(COURTESY OF THE PHOTOGRAPHER)

NOPD was already known for its brutality. New Orleans cops have made it into movies like *Easy Rider* and *The Big Easy*, without much exaggeration. In 1990, Adolph Archie, a black man suspected of killing a white officer, was stomped to death on his way to the hospital. One hundred cops converged on the hospital, broadcasting threats over their police radios. Citizens' complaints against the police, ranging from rudeness to brutality, already reached an all-time high at the start of 1993, with 1,200 complaints logged against a police force of 1,500.

And in 1994, forty of that year's crimes, from rape to murder, were committed by police officers.

The rest, of course, were committed by criminals.

Tourists come to New Orleans to get drunk, to get weird, and to get laid. They also come to eat and, some of them say, to dance and hear *le jazz*. They get that. And plenty more. Sometimes they get rolled and killed. Sometimes they get arrested for running a red light and put in jail with thieves and killers. You can't ask for anything better in America. To get all those thrills separately you'd have to go to Belfast, to Bangkok, to Haiti, to Paris, and you'd still have to come to New Orleans for the music.

When the rich, the famous, the bored, the weird, and just plain fugitives fantasize about disappearing, they inevitably think of New Orleans. Over the years—the past three hundred years—countless alienated souls have made it to the French Quarter. They may have been reported "missing" back in their boring hometowns, but they've never looked back. There is a whole class of people here who, for lack of a pithier term, I'll call "people who never left." They span the range. During the Tomato Festival when they elect the Tomato Queen, a sixtyish woman dressed like a tomato with long green tights appears. She circulates among the throngs, poo-pooing the "real" Tomato Queen who is, usually, a fresh-faced Creole beauty from the Acadian parishes. "She ain't the Tomato Queen! I am!" she proclaims haughtily. "I been the queen for twenty years now when I left husband and childrens in Georgia and came down here. Never went back, never looked back. I'd love to talk to you, darling, but I still got good legs! I gotta circulate!" And circulate she does, the one and only queen, red and green and without regrets.

Francis Ford Coppola has a house in the French Quarter. Bob Dylan lives uptown on a gated street. My kid went to a birthday party next door to Dylan's. They were playing Blind Melon and the Smashing Pumpkins and Dylan called and told them to turn down the racket. My friend Harry Shearer sneaks into town a lot but always comes for Jazz Fest in March. One day we walked past two guys with huge bellies spilling from under T-shirts three sizes too small with JAZZ FEST 1992 written on them. They greeted Harry effusively and puffed themselves up. When they had passed I asked him who they were. "Executives at Disney and Warner Brothers," he said. Or maybe it was the other way around. In any case, those two hadn't been out of a suit all year, but here they were, in New Orleans. Oh, boy! I could just hear the one telling the other: "I always plan to gain fifty pounds over the weekend. I'll work it off for the next six months!" (Which is real dialogue I overheard on a New Orleans–bound plane last week.) Julia Roberts and Lyle Lovett fell in love dancing at Cafe Brazil. The Iguanas were playing. Those two didn't gain an ounce. They did the other New Orleans thing. The list of celebrities who like to disappear at least part-time in New Orleans is long and growing. Dorian Bennett, real estate agent to the stars, whispered a few more names to me at a party but swore me to secrecy until the deeds are done. I couldn't have remembered them anyway. I *do* recall the huge crabs on ice and the oysters en brochette, the mimosas, and the jazz trio. Two tall girls were dancing with each other. An off-duty policeman was posted outside the gate. On my way to the bathroom I passed an impressive security system with a lit console blinking like a hundred-red-eyed beast. I'm not even sure whose house it was or what the party was for. A celebrity or two may have been hanging around but I was settling into the fleur-heavy lassitude of a New Orleans night and my thoughts were reaching for the real stars. And this is Reason Number One why celebrities adore New Orleans: nobody seems to recognize them and if they do they make no fuss over them. New Orleanians are polite. (And their memories are sieves.) New Orleans guarantees anonymity. Reason Number

Two is real estate. Cheap mansions abound: Greek Revival, Southern plantation, fifties *moderne*, you name it. Dorian can get it for you and then you can be inducted into the new religion of the South: restoration. There is nothing celebrities love more than a cheap (but expensive) new religion. New Orleans is the Rome of Restoration. *Pace, Savannah.*

The native aristocrats whose faces adorn the weighty society page of the *New Orleans Times-Picayune* know the score. Their parties are well policed, their dogs well trained. A gentleman I know packs a pistol in the inner pocket of his tuxedo jacket. But besides these elementary precautions, the windows of their chateaus are brightly lit and the hoi polloi can squish their noses against them while the balls whirl. Newcomers may think that they are in Venice or Saint Tropez.

Fifty paces or so from the *grand manses* of the *nouveau* New Orleanians, following the azalea bushes upriver, the decay begins. At first, there is no particular distinction in the styles, but there are boarded-up windows and gaping doorways and the street life gets more interesting. In truth, these are distinct and culturally rich areas that have been hit by the general ills of urban America. Many of these 'hoods are now subject to intense gentrification that takes place sometimes overnight. A joint called Jackie's II, on Magazine Street, became Jacqueline's Paris Baby Clothes one day. Jackie's II was a lovely community bar that had free spaghetti on Tuesdays and free fish fry on Fridays. Jackie herself, a warmhearted black woman in her fifties, took care of people and made sure that all the news fit to whisper passed by her first. She kept the crack dealers out of there and was on pretty good terms with the police. When Jacqueline's Paris Baby Clothes retired her, the bereft customers dispersed. Across the street, the crack dealers made a stand and multiplied. When the poor neighborhoods are attacked, the poor get pushed into the housing projects, where the real troublemakers are. The housing projects, particularly Desire, St.

Thomas, and Fisher, are shooting galleries. The drug dealers rule them at night. Automatic weapon fire is their *kleine nacht music*.

The police officers guarding the crowd at the Royal Street Gallery where I was supposed to meet a friend were being paid by the gallery to make sure that riffraff stayed away from the patrons. It was a velvety evening when the air feels like skin. The sweet sounds of a street band were floating on the soft breeze. It was the kind of air, a friend of mine once said, that feels like you're being kissed.

There was a commotion in front of the art gallery, but nothing that would get a New Orleans policeman excited. A hefty gaggle of gawkers watched a man wearing Tony Lamas boots, a painting under his arm, wearing a ten-gallon hat and nothing else, get into a De-Lorean. I had never seen one so I got as close as I could. They really have those funny doors that go up like an angel's wings. The mostly naked man threw the painting in the backseat and gallantly lifted a wing for an elegant daughter of Louisiana, clad demurely in a later-Scarlett O'Hara gown. Next day I heard the story from her own mouth. Her name is Tiffany and she was still bubbly after only a few hours' sleep. It seems that this man had walked into the gallery where she worked and demanded a date. When she demurred, he purchased a $25,000 work of art with cash and disrobed. "And let me tell you, darling," my mouthpiece crooned, "it wasn't his *cash* that got my attention!" The date had apparently gone on swimmingly until another *belle fille* showed up in the suite at the Windsor Court. "That sort of broke my concentration, if you'd know what I mean," said Tiffany meaningfully. I saw how that might, but my friend, not one to concede defeat, said that she'd simply ordered more Dom Perignon. And there was the coke, of course. Sparkling, fat white lines snaking the whole length of a big wall mirror they'd taken down. Peruvian flake. The best.

And then she cut off her story. Maybe she simply didn't *recall*. Many New Orleans *jeune filles en fleur* suffer from this affliction.

I have seen enough naked men in New Orleans to be blasé about it. At Mardi Gras, the whole French Quarter goes on a binge of exhibitionism. It used to be a few tits here and there only ten years ago, but it's gotten epidemic. "Show your tits!" was the cry of the plebeians who begged under balconies for a glimpse of royal flesh. Later, it was the balconies that dangled beads to the plebes, making them exhibit for plastic. But then, in the past few years, everyone started taking off everything at the merest raise of an eyebrow. At a gay bar just this side of "the lavender line" on Bourbon Street, six men were dancing nude on the bartop with the doors wide open and the tourists from Minneapolis couldn't load their cameras fast enough.

Flesh, champagne, art, and DeLoreans are an eighties combination, but the eighties (whether the 1880s or the 1980s) have never gone away here. Neither has any other age to which thrills this city took. You can walk into barrooms where it's the forties. Or the fifties. The jukebox, the mirrors over the bar, the pickled eggs in the jars, the decorations, and the people are all period perfect. Every establishment offers its time warp without fuss. You can be any time in New Orleans. It's preserved. Something in the river-heavy air keeps the flavors of various times for the pleasure of those who never climbed out of them. Everything else rots: houses, flesh, books. But the spirits of times past stay eerily present. The crime-ridden St. Thomas housing projects, for instance, are firmly situated on historical grounds. Here is how they looked in 1861 to a writer of the *True Delta*, a New Orleans newspaper: "St. Thomas Street is keeping up its ancient reputation, especially that portion of it which boasts of Corduroy Alley. The inhabitants of the Alley appear for the most part to be an intemperate and blood-thirsty set, who are never contented unless engaged in broils, foreign or domestic, such as the breaking of a stranger's pate or the blacking of a loving spouse's eye." *Plus ça change.*

New Orleans joined gangland America late. Drive-by shootings, executions of rival drug dealers, random murders, car jackings, and crack took some time to get here from Los Angeles. The local style, while certainly violent, was far from systematic. But by 1993, America arrived. A horrifying crime wave engulfed the city. The newspaper began keeping score of daily murders. Bookies were taking bets on the number. In 1994, New Orleans became the murder capital of the United States, with 425 killings.

Len Davis, the "Desire Terrorist," was known to the police before he became one. He was arrested twice in 1985, once for battery and urinating in public, and once on a municipal warrant on an undisclosed charge. It's worth noting that urinating in public in New Orleans is a long-standing tradition and hardly worth mention if it were not for the local flavor. Old cities, like Paris, for instance, are vast pissoirs. In 1987, while training to be a police officer, Davis was kicked out of the academy for disciplinary reasons. He resumed training a few months later and was turned loose on his former Desire Project neighbors with the law on his side. In no time at all, he acquired an extensive history of citizen complaints against him. He was suspended for fifty-one days in 1992 for hitting a woman on the head with a flashlight. Charges of brutality, physical intimidation, and theft were lodged against him, but no action was taken. On October 13, 1994, Kim Groves, a mother of three who was going to testify against him for pistol-whipping one of her son's friends, was shot in the head. The killer, Paul "Cool" Handy, blew her away on orders from Davis.

Davis had barked his explicit orders to Handy over a cellular phone: "Get that whore!" He described for the killer what the woman wore. For the next several hours, Handy and his sidekick, Damon Causey, shadowed Kim Groves and talked with Davis on his cellular phone. Finally, Handy pulled the trigger. Davis declared himself satisfied and the three of them celebrated their success. The day after Groves's death, Davis got on his cellular and discussed killing another witness against him. Davis asked Handy "to cool off" to see if the person complained again, and if he did "it would be rock-a-bye-baby."

But there is a real question of whether Kim Groves had to die. The whole time that the killer cop was instructing his henchmen, the FBI was listening in. Davis was at the center of a yearlong federal investigation into the cocaine trade in New Orleans. The FBI had set up a sting, using tons of real cocaine and real cash. Len Davis and at least nine other police officers were engaged in guarding and moving the cash and the cocaine for FBI agents posing as drug dealers. At one point, Davis and his gang considered killing the "dealers," but trust was reestablished in a surreal scene, worthy of the city where nakedness is an institution. According to U.S. Attorney Eddie Jordan, "The undercover agent . . . stripped before the police officers to show that he was not wired at the time. The police officers did the same, and this was captured on videotape."

I wouldn't be surprised if this tape showed up in French Quarter bars for sale, like many other amateur videos shot in New Orleans by voyeurs.

At the time of Kim Groves's murder, the FBI stood poised to nab as many as twenty officers who may have been involved with the Davis gang. Neil Gallagher, the FBI agent in charge, denied that the FBI could have stopped the killing. He said that the cellular phone conversations "were spread out over a ten-hour period and were intermingled with many other discussions concerning their protection activity." These conversations, according to Gallagher, were pretty "cryptic." But a look at the transcripts reveals that the murder order was anything but cryptic: "Get that whore!" What could that possibly mean? It is far more likely that the FBI, coming close to touching the bottom of the nearly bottomless pit that is the NOPD, got too greedy. Faced with a second possible murder, they reluctantly shut down the can of worms with only ten of the slimers out of it.

New Orleans is an island that floats on the brackish swill of a complicated past and emanates an intoxicating scent of decay and promise. Here is the pudendum of North America, the last stop of the Mississippi River before it surrenders its flow to the Gulf of Mexico. The Mississippi River is not a happy river: it sings the blues of toxic pollution, the shackles put on it by the Army Corps of Engineers, the pain of levees and dams, and above all, its sad story of frustrated love for the swift and young Atchafalaya River. The Mississippi has been attempting for one century to join up with the young Atchafalaya, but the Corps has prevented it with the biggest locks in its arsenal. Sooner or later they will join because what the Old Man River wants the OMR gets. The joining would shorten its way to the gulf by 120 miles. But its new course would leave New Orleans high and dry. New Orleans without the Mississippi! Unimaginable. This is one more sorrowful piece of knowledge that gnaws irrevocably at the unconscious of the natives. And so, like Venice, this is a doomed city.

The Mississippi, in its journey from the heartland to the gulf, brings here all of America's sins and secrets. It's a journey of downflow ethics. A few years ago in Minneapolis they busted a candidate for the city council for distributing Twinkies to an old folks home. They slapped him with two weeks of community service for attempted vote buying. At the same time in New Orleans, Governor Edwin Edwards was handing bags full of cash to Vegas boys in the lobby of a downtown hotel to pay his gambling debts. The governor was registered in the hotel under the name Lee. The Chinese name was part of Edwin's famous sense of humor. When the citizenry was polled as to the propriety of

the governor's handing cash to Vegas boys in a hotel lobby where he
was registered under a Chinese pseudonym, the majority opined that
there was no harm done if it was his own money.

The Mississippi River stretches from the guilty Twinkies of Minnesota to the insouciant cash of New Orleans. Along the shores these
days one can follow the decay of virtue in America. But let the citizens
of the upper reaches not feel too smug: New Orleans is a lot more fun
than Minneapolis.

On the Moonwalk by the river in downtown New Orleans, a saxo-
phonist lets loose with a melancholy rendition of Charlie Parker's
"Mood." A few tourists gawk at him misty-eyed because he fits exactly
into that jazz-musician-shaped hole in their heads that they brought
with them from the Midwest. In truth, the man isn't bad. He's loose,
playful, and knows exactly what he's dishing up. He's a good-looking
black man in his midfifties, with a salt-and-pepper beard. The sax case
at his feet is stickered with European decals. He's played Paris, Am-
sterdam, and Barcelona. The sax case is open and quickly filling with
fives. His name, or pseudonym, is Alexander.

In January 1994, a twenty-three-year-old Italian beauty named
Ylenia Carrisi disappeared in New Orleans. Ylenia was the Vanna
White of Italy, a letter turner on the Italian version of *The Wheel of
Fortune*. She was also the daughter of Romina Power and Al Bano, a
couple known as the Sonny and Cher of Italy. Her grandfather was the
American actor Tyrone Power. In addition to her celebrity pedigree,
Ylenia was a blond-haired, green-eyed siren who loved travel, adventure, and art. Something of a latter-day beatnik, she had carried her
bedroll through Mexico and Central America. She had read Kerouac,
was enamored of *le jazz*, and was writing a novel. In New Orleans, she
hung out with drifters and musicians in Jackson Square. On a previous
visit she had befriended a saxophone player called Pachakan. She re-

turned to the city from Belize because, according to her mother, "she fell in love with the city . . ." and came back "to find characters for a book she was writing." One of these was a musician named Alexander Masakela who, according to her parents, "put her under some kind of spell." She lived with him in a flophouse on lower St. Charles Avenue.

The police arrested Alexander on an unrelated charge and held him for eleven days before a judge ordered his release. Police spokesmen claimed that a woman who jumped into the Mississippi River near the Moonwalk on January 6 was Ylenia Carrisi. The existence of the woman who jumped into the river was attested to only by the testimony of a night watchman, who claimed to have witnessed the jump. But his description of the jumper did not match Ylenia Carrisi's. The $150,000 reward offered for Ylenia's safe return still stands. The body was never found and no one was held responsible for her disappearance.

Jackson Square, where Ylenia liked to hang out, is flanked on two sides by the Pontalba Apartments, said to be the first apartment buildings in the United States. They were built in the eighteenth century by Baroness Pontalba, who had fallen on hard times and was compelled to rent. Across from these now chic digs is the Cabildo Museum, the former headquarters of the Spanish administration where slaves were sent for whippings. More memorably, here is where the Louisiana Purchase was signed in 1803. The purchase of Louisiana and most of the United States west of the Mississippi, from Napoleon by Thomas Jefferson, was the best deal the Republic ever made. Displayed in the courtyard of this museum complex is also an object of great importance to understanding the psyche of New Orleans: a confederate submarine. This blimplike object is utterly mysterious. Intended to somehow skewer Yankee ships on the Mississippi, it housed two sailors who propelled it along the muddy bottom with their feet. The first (and last) confederate submarine never worked. As such, it is a valiant expression of the South's (and the city's) delight in unworkably mysterious situations.

Facing the square is St. Louis Cathedral, the premiere birth-to-death sanctum sanctorum of prominent New Orleanians. Facing the St. Louis Cathedral is a round bronze plaque commemorating the visit of Pope Paul VI to New Orleans in 1987. When a hot-dog vendor isn't resting his cart on it, the little Pope memorial is an excellent spot for a panoramic view of the square. On weekends, Jackson Square is filled to bursting with clowns, fire-eaters, mimes, break-dancers, musicians, and scores of tarot readers, crystal gazers, gigolos, filles-de-joies, and, of course, tourists. A narrow alley to the side of St. Louis Cathedral is called the Pirates' Alley because privateers were reputed to have conducted business there. It now smells strongly of centuries-old urine, like Paris. A bit farther up this cobblestone path is the Faulkner House, where the young William F. penned his first novel, *Soldier's Pay*. It is now a bookstore, literary salon, and headquarters of *The Double Dealer* magazine. Faulkner, who spent all his early and later life in Oxford, Mississippi, was powerfully stamped by New Orleans. New Orleans, like Oxford, is *in* the Deep South, but its connections reach way beyond its geography.

Jackson Square in its manifold complexity mirrors the city. Represented here are the various administrations, foremost the Spanish, French, and American. The architecture of the French Quarter is primarily Spanish, but the laissez-faire mentality and cheerful corruption is French. For a hundred years or so anarchy was the city's modus vivendi. At one point, privateers, in collusion with the temporal powers, pretty much ran the city. The pirate Jean Laffite is said to have insured the triumph of the United States over the British in the War of 1812. (There are two movies to prove it.) Justice was often haphazard and the citizens were known to take it into their own hands. In 1893, a mob dissatisfied with the verdict of a jury on the matter of the murder of the city's police chief broke into the Parish Prison in Congo Square and lynched eleven Italians who had just been acquitted of the deed. Their rallying cry, "Who Killa Da Chief?," was used for decades thereafter as an insult toward Italians, adding to the rich lingo of disparagement that the city's varied ethnicities employed on one another. The Irish of the Irish Channel ragged on the Italians, the descendants of the French and the Spanish had little tolerance for the Uptown Americans, and mulattoes took pains to distinguish between shades of blackness.

The animosities of the honest citizens were undergirded by a solid criminal infrastructure. Thieves, cutthroats, gamblers, con men, prostitutes, drug addicts, and drunks have always claimed a good-sized chunk of turf in New Orleans. In a letter from New Orleans on January 27, 1857, James Sterling, an English traveler, noted with amazement that in the Fifth District Court alone there were then pending fourteen cases of murder, twenty of shooting and stabbing, and 340 of assault and battery. "The proportion of crime to the population," he wrote, "is, to a European, perfectly astounding."

The above item is culled from a book called *The French Quarter* by Herbert Asbury, first published in 1936. Asbury goes on to note that in the mid-nineteenth century, "the criminals and ruffians whose unchecked depredations had transformed New Orleans into what the Criminal Sheriff so graphically described as 'a perfect Hell on earth' found refuge and amusement in the scores of cheap groggeries, dance-houses, bordellos, low taverns and coffeehouses, concert-saloons and barrel-houses with which the Vieux Carré and the area above Canal Street were literally crowded."

In parts of the French Quarter and at the edges of neighborhoods the lines blur. Nobody has counted the number of bars lately in New Orleans, but it's a fair assumption that they have always outnumbered such establishments anywhere else in America. What is certain is that many of them stay open all night and always have, which gives New Orleans the distinction of having had the longest sleepless night in American history. My friend Jason Berry told me that Tom Wolfe said that New York in the eighties was good for a novel every time you opened the morning paper. "New Orleans is like that now," said Jason. True, it's rich now, but it always was. The line between criminals and the police and the politicians was blurred more often than not. Top to bottom, the roles and uniforms could change like night and day. The colorful careers of Huey P. Long and of his brother Earl K. Long, governors of Louisiana, are exemplary in this regard. When Huey P. Long was assassinated in 1935, the heirs looked for the "deduct box," a cash cache containing the ten percent tithe state employees paid directly to Huey. "The deduct box" was never found. Brother Earl had a passionate liaison with the stripper Blaize Starr and was quite familiar with the underworld of New Orleans late-night joints. He was also put away in a mental hospital but freed himself because he fired the chief of the hospital, who was his subordinate.

Now and then, quite often in fact, the good citizens claimed to have had enough. Anticorruption campaigns swept rotten politicians from office, forced a few cops to change sides, and routed gamblers out of the state. The notorious Louisiana State Lottery was dismantled at the start of the century by the grandfather of our current governor, Mike Foster. Foster, like his grandfather, claims to want to do something about the growing choke-hold of gambling on the state and the city.

Gambling found in Louisiana a rich soil of predisposed suckers. The French had been notorious gamblers. Stories of lost fortunes, duels, and suicide are part of the native romance. Riverboat gamblers disembarked here and fleeced the natives until they had to flee. Wagering is woven into the fabric. The Cajuns of southern Louisiana are fond of cards, particularly the game called *bourrée*, which can quickly involve substantial sums. Foster's predecessor, Governor Edwin Edwards, a Cajun from Crowley, Louisiana, elected four times, indicted just as many and found just as many times innocent, was a gambler. He played poker in the governor's mansion with people whose mere appearance would have offended Minnesotans. He rolled the dice in Vegas for big money. And, wonder of wonders, he won! His dream, as he romantically put it, was to bring casino gambling to Louisiana so that all might have his thrills. His dream became reality in the succeeding administration of Buddy Roemer, a weak-kneed transitional ruler whose reign was sandwiched between two Edwards administrations. Roemer signed into law many forms of gambling, including video poker and the lottery. The New Orleans land casino, Harrah's, will be the second largest in the world (the first is on Indian land in Connecticut) when it opens.

With big gambling came big trouble. Until now, corruption had always found a peaceable level, a balance between greed and gravy. When the money had been relatively small what was bought stayed relatively reasonable. But with the arrival of the big boys with the big money the local pols started seeing dancing sugar plums. The rush to the trough became frantic. The sloppiness ended eventually when, in 1995, the FBI released surveillance tapes that implicated about half the Louisiana legislature in trading pro-gambling votes for campaign contributions. The surprise, for most citizens, was how little it cost to buy a vote. Even one hundred bucks would get you *something* in Baton Rouge. The shadow of the mob always flitted delicately in the corners of legislative smoke rooms, but in the rush to pull in their markers, mobsters became indiscreet. Many legislators decided not to run for reelection. The mob also lost a few of its marginal soldiers to the law in the rush to control the insanely profitable video-poker-machine business.

Something changed in Louisiana when gambling became law in

1994. While some of the events I am about to describe may not appear directly related, they share an atmosphere. Take, for instance, the utterly bizarre case of the former Baton Rouge mayor Pat Screen, who died of a drug overdose in a second-rate New Orleans hotel. A former football player, a reform Republican (a rarity in the land of Dixiecrats), he projected a squeaky-clean image. Prior to his death, a companion ran all over town trying to pawn or sell Screen's football ring for two thousand dollars. She was unsuccessful because she returned to the room with the ring. The ex-mayor's death remained briefly unreported while his wife and children were notified and allowed to take the body back to Baton Rouge. But why did he need so much cash? Drugs are not very expensive. Was there a gambling debt? The mystery continues.

Antoine Saacks was the city's top homicide cop, a twenty-eight-year veteran of the New Orleans Police. In 1994 he was forced to resign amidst charges ranging from theft to associating with mobsters. But his real offense was his work on behalf of United Gaming, Inc. of Las Vegas, which paid him $325,000 to persuade businessmen to install video poker machines in their establishments. New Orleans policemen are quite adept at persuasion. The entire vice squad was disbanded when it was reported that officers regularly raided cash registers at city bars, strip joints, and massage parlors. Before it was disbanded, the vice squad was touted as an elite unit handpicked by then-superintendent Arnesta Taylor. Other officers shook down businesses for protection. It was no wonder that Saacks's men were extremely successful. There are very few bars or restaurants in New Orleans that do not sport several video poker machines now.

Saacks fought the charges with all his might, insisting that everything he did was legal. He was a charismatic figure well known to, among others, Hollywood producers. Saacks's troops provided security for moviemakers in New Orleans, rerouting traffic, guarding equipment, and procuring services. All this in return for cash, of course and, occasionally, small movie roles for the city's finest. In the end, Saacks's various activities cast too much shadow over him and he lost his fight for reinstatement.

Antoine Saacks, the city's chief white cop, and Len Davis, the ghetto tough, stole the headlines in the fall of 1994, but other police crimes, from grave to trivial, were having their day. Sgt. Henry Morel was sentenced to eighteen months in prison for public bribery and shakedowns at French Quarter bars and strip joints. Officers John Martin and Richard Burgess were convicted of robbing a man in a pub. Officer Marc Galbreth stole a credit card and went on a shopping spree. Sgt. Edward Massina was guilty of forcing a woman into his car to perform oral sex. Two officers were convicted of raping an underage girl in a hotel room. Officers were accused of stealing cars. Another gang within the NOPD was accused of filing false insurance claims for accidents that never happened. And in the middle of all this, the long-suffering citizens of New Orleans continued to complain that the cops were in a bad mood.

No wonder. The national media caught on to the doings here and it didn't help matters. CBS's *Sixty Minutes* broadcast a searing report on the NOPD on October 30, 1994. The young new mayor of New Orleans, Marc Morial, promised tough reforms and changes. He appointed Richard Pennington, a former Washington, D.C., cop, police superintendent. Chief Pennington promised to stomp out corruption, brutality, complaints, and low morale. It didn't look like things could get any worse. But they did. Exhausted New Orleanians would have gladly called on the Carnival gods to help them forget, if such were possible. Mardi Gras is the balm that unites everyone in the city, black and white, rich and poor, old and young. Sexes, races, ages, change form. Identities become a matter of costuming skill and talent. African dance and voodoo ritual combines with Catholic pageantry and native

exuberance to produce a genuinely New World bacchanalia. The composition of Carnival societies comprises the true social fabric of New
Orleans. African Indians, Creole aristocrats, homosexual esthetes, and
hallucinating outsiders come together in a sea swell of ritual and oblivion. Surprisingly good-natured for decades, Mardi Gras was also a test
to the crowd-control skills of the local police, one of its few points of
pride. But even Carnival had been touched by the malaise of over-
articulation in America. Councilwoman Dorothy Mae Taylor pushed
through the city council a resolution mandating the integration of the
old-line white Carnival Krewes. While this may mean nothing to the
rest of the world, in New Orleans it was an epic issue that shook
the very gumbo under our feet. But as the shadow of sobriety passed
over the shape-shifting intoxication of Mardi Gras, a great unease fell
over the city.

In the midst of the quotidian horror, something else came to the
fore to top the cake. On April 30, 1995, the *New Orleans Times-
Picayune* published the photographs and available biographies of
twenty-four young women and men who may have been the victims
of a serial killer operating in New Orleans since 1991. The bodies of
two women were discovered in a desolate stretch just outside New
Orleans in May of 1995. One of the women, a money changer at the
temporary Harrah's casino, was the girlfriend of a Seventh District pa-
trolman, Victor Gant, who had been seen leaving with her the night
she disappeared. Gant, who was subsequently fired for violating department regulations, is still being investigated for two of the murders.

Human bones are no news in New Orleans where voodoo has been
making use of them for centuries. The grave of Marie Laveau, voodoo
priestess, at the St. Louis Cemetery No. 1, is often plied with suspect
offerings in the middle of the night. Horror stories are told of houses
in the French Quarter and Uptown where ghosts have returned to point

out the location of their own bones. A member of the inefficient Internal Investigation Unit of the NOPD said, about Antoinette Frank, that, "she flew below radar." Below that same radar, swarming like a cloud of swamp insects, were other deranged and corrupt killer cops.

With many citizens afraid to trust the police, thugs of the lowest kind were acting with impunity. While the New Orleans city and tourist bureaus were doing their best to emphasize the pleasures of the bread pudding in whiskey sauce at Commander's Palace or the shrimp creole at Coop's (my favorite), it was hard to wave off the onslaught of daily news. On the sixth of November 1995, a car jacker shot a young mother and her baby. He shot and killed the baby deliberately, in the head. The killer and his accomplice were caught quickly, turned in by the horrified neighbors. At the funeral, the baby's mother, who survived, said, "New Orleans is the most beautiful city in America, the most historic city, and the city with the most potential. But it is a city with a sickness."

During the gubernatorial campaign, Mike Foster advocated arming every citizen in the state, and called New Orleans a jungle, a comment with racist overtones. If you are going to add guns to a population already bristling with them, things will get worse. But then, this wasn't anything new either. Herbert Asbury describes a similar situation in the 1870s: "No permit was required for the possession of firearms, and men of all classes habitually carried weapons to protect their lives and property, although no one seems to have been in any real danger from a pistol or revolver in the hands of the average citizen." Mainly because none of them could shoot straight.

To express their pleasure at the end of years, New Orleanians discharge their myriad weapons into the sky. The year 1994 ended with two shootings: Amy Silberman, a tourist from Massachusetts, was killed by a bullet from the sky while she was waiting for the fireworks to start. My friend Gil Helmick was hit by the same kind of random bullet that entered his chest an inch below his heart. He lived, and he became fiercely active in trying to stop the shooting. He put a poster with the faces of hundreds of people wounded by such shootings over the years in every citizen's hand.

In a touching display of whimsy, one hundred residents of the Bywater area who were victims of crime held a ceremony invoking the voodoo god Ogoun Le Flambeau to rid the city of the evils of crack cocaine. The priestess chanted, offered rum and cigars, and her followers pounded the drums. The few older black residents watching from their doorways shook their heads in wonder. The voodoo practitioners were all white. The priestess herself was from Kennebunkport, Maine. But then who knows? Something has to work. The problems of New Orleans are the problems of urban America. There are bad cops in Philadelphia and street killers in Detroit. But the peculiar intensity of what we have experienced is colored by a violent history that took a long time and a lot of forgetfulness to become romantic. A French Quarter bar owner posted the tallies of murders in Boston and in New Orleans, comparing the two cities. But it was not a fair comparison. Some of our stories are as murky as the Mississippi and almost as old as Old Man River.

Listen to the low, mournful moans of barges pulling chemicals down the Mississippi. You will hear the sound of broken glass and two voices raised in anger. Stella and Stanley are at it again. Listen carefully and you might hear a new wave of flowers break into bloom over by Prytania Street, where stately Gothic mansions cater to their ghosts. A bar lets out its music-stuffed customers who spill noisily into the street. By six A.M., the birds of New Orleans explode into song. You will hear a mockingbird with a vast repertoire that includes car alarms, slamming doors, moaning barges, saxophones, and automatic weapons. The mockingbird ought to be our totem now: it mirrors Sorry Humanity without much understanding it.

The gang seated in the window at Molly's on Decatur Street was more than usually frisky: it was one of those vanilla-ice-cream New Orleans afternoons and there were more than the bearable number of *fleurs* partrembling past. It would take a whole pastel palette to put them into perspective: suffice it to say they trembled and ruffled, all silk, satin, organdy, swish, swagger, and blush. Nor were these *fleurs'* genders so very clear, this being the French Quarter, the place where cross-dressing is like beignets and café au lait. Not an everyday kind of thing, but pretty much routine. Following the gender-uncertain *fleurs*, nouveau freaks tumbled past Molly's: they weren't just more numerous, but also more pierced, more painted, more scarred. A human painting fastened by a nose bone to its female counterpart (who differed only in texture) rattled by at the end of a silver chain. A boy with a photographically precise tattoo of Sly Stone on his shoulder stopped to call out to no one in particular, "Open the Archives!"

The window gang could barely focus on anything for longer than a second before its collective attention was dragged through the gargoyled mud of yet another volley of human vanity. Inside Molly's, at the piano, Professor Big Stuff, his silver ponytail flying, was taking a survey prior to launching into a spirited version of Tom Lehrer's "Masochism Blues." "How many masochists here?" he shouted. Several hands went up, including the delicate fingers of the Chinese girl who'd been perching in light gloom at the end of the bar for the past hour drinking one Tom Collins after another. "Light or heavy?" shouted the professor. "Oh, light," she said.

Everywhere else this cumulation of incidents would have signaled the coming of spring or the casting of a major motion picture, but in New Orleans it meant only that Mardi Gras was coming. And with it came the people. More people than one imagines possible. People with

KERRI W. MCCAFFETY: *Mardi Gras*
(COURTESY OF THE PHOTOGRAPHER)

an idée fixe, parrot, peacock, or loon people, here to voyeurize, display, boogie, strut, prance, and lose it. These are Americans for the most part, mind you, people who in their hometowns are bankers and accountants. Here, they become something inexplicably deranged. A young mother, towing a husband whose leopard-skin loincloth did not obscure the sober-minded pate at the top of his corporate head, told a television reporter: "The kids are at the hotel with a baby-sitter and I'm here to show my breasts if anyone asks." The reporter asked. She pulled the velveteen tank top right off her considerable endowments. They wouldn't be on the ten o'clock news, but the expression on her face would. An indescribable mien that says, approximately, "Take that, Kalamazoo!"

A *baby-sitter!* howled the window gang. Jeezus! A baby-sitter in New Orleans! At Mardi Gras! And just to prove the point, a gaggle of baby-sitters clad in nunlike garments led forth a passel of bediapered adult babes sucking on rum-filled baby bottles. This is not to cast aspersions: somebody's got to mind the children in the city whose motto is, "If you can reach the bar, you can have it!"

The first to march this year was the Krewe de Vieux Carré, which is subdivided into the Krewe of Underwear, the Krewe of the Mystick Corpse, and the Krewe of the Comatose. The themes of this venerable organization—the only one allowed to march through the French Quarter proper—was "Unnaturally New Orleans" this year. The theme is different every year, but it is usually political satire. This year's bizarre theme baffled even the members who couldn't figure out what in the world was unnatural in the Babylon on the Bayou. Some suggested adopting the habits and mannerisms of a small Midwestern town, which would have been most unnatural, but even the thought caused drowsiness. The Krewe of Comatose, to which I belong, decided to go for the politically relevant. We decided to perform a requiem for the Rivergate. The Rivergate was an extravagant seventies-style convention

hall with a roof like the hat of a flying nun. It was pretty daring ar-
chitecturally at the time it was built, but then it started leaking. When
Big Gambling came to town, Harrah's Casino proposed to turn the
Rivergate into a gambling hall, but the city required Harrah to demolish it first and then build something else. New Orleanians, who
laughed at the building for years, became suddenly nostalgic. But you
can't fight Harrah's and city hall with nostalgia so the Rivergate came
down, roof and all, to make room for something so ugly there aren't
even jokes for it yet.

The Krewe of Comatose, hundred-strong dressed in black, wearing
foam hats in the shape of the doomed Rivergate, marched in the rain
past the still-standing roof. A brass band filled the night with traditional second-line funeral tunes. A police cruiser just behind the
band—which brought up the rear of the parade—turned on its sirens,
trying to drown out the dirges. When an outraged marcher attempted
to reason with the cop, he came tumbling out with his stick raised
high. Mardi Gras, of course, is the worst time in the world for cops to
be in a bad mood. Riot-type situations abound. Naked people throw
themselves off balconies into the arms of mobs. Drunks and druggies
howl in the middle of the road and vault over moving vehicles. The
population in the city triples. An uncool cop can be match to gasoline.
So far, Mardi Gras has been a surprisingly benign festival, with some
gross exceptions now and then. It's a miracle, or a series of them. New
Orleans is a Catholic city, God looks after it. By Ash Wednesday He's
exhausted. So is everyone else. The belligerent cop pulled back his
stick. This time. The Krewe of Comatose marched on, wailing for modern architecture.

Musics (pl.), New Orleans's greatest asset, are in particular bloom
around Mardi Gras. Every parade hires bands, every hall is filled. The
scene used to happen in little dives like the Maple Leaf Bar, but lately
the sharks of big entertainment have been goose-stepping in. The

House of Blues, the Hard Rock Cafe, and Planet Hollywood have all established beachheads. The dives are still going strong, but the tourists do the sardine thing in the bricky new phonies.

Being a New Orleanian is getting to be tough. A polite people, the natives have always suffered the intrusion of tourism with honeyed Southern resentment. However, the combination of Big Gambling, Big Crime, Big Stars, and Big Entertainment, in short, Big Money, may prove too much. We aren't yet ready to desert our dreamy burg yet, but if the Disneying continues, we may have to retreat, leaving an empty shell. Or we can fight, after we finish this mint julep here.

WALKER EVANS: *Roadside Stand Near Birmingham*
(J. PAUL GETTY MUSEUM, LOS ANGELES)

The South, or What Surrounds New Orleans

In the South there were men of delicate fancy, urbane instinct and aristocratic manner—in brief, superior men—in brief, gentry. To politics, their chief diversion, they brought active and original minds. It was there that nearly all the political theories we still cherish and suffer under came to birth. It was there that the crude dogmatism of New England was refined and humanized. It was there, above all, that some attention was given to the art of living—that life got beyond and above the state of a mere infliction and became an exhilarating experience. A certain notable spaciousness was in the ancient Southern scheme of things. The *Ur*-Confederate had leisure. He liked to toy with ideas. He was hospitable and tolerant. He had the vague thing that we call culture.

—H. L. Mencken, "The Sahara of the Bozart"

On the other hand, there was Royal Montgomery, who humped like a bunny all over the state, but whose blood was of the bluest. As the Dear Old Thing explained on the way to the Richard Evelyn Byrd Flying Field, the South is made up of old blood and old money; old blood and new money; and that especially revered category, old blood and no money.

—Florence King, *Southern Ladies and Gentlemen*

Many, many years ago, in the inflated seventies, when both ideas and money were quickly losing value, a man named Jimmy Carter rode out of the South holding aloft a banner that said, THE NEW SOUTH. But before we could quite figure out what was new about it, the Confederacy rejected the notion, and we settled back into what we knew best: the close examination of our wounds. The New South seemed to imply somehow that we'd gotten over our resentment at losing the War, or over what we knew that we knew, if you'd know what I mean. Thank God for David Duke and Pat Buchanan, men who'll never let us forget.

—Patti Rankin-Cole, *Too Much Home*

"And the river," I asked with a smile in my voice. "How's it doing?"

"The river's fine. Just fine. There was a delegation from China in here recently and I took them over the levee to look at our river. They said it was awesome."

—Tom Dent, *Southern Journeys*

A Transylvanian in Dixieland

N ew Orleans is not the South."
I hear this often, from people who spend a few days in the
city. Well, it is and it isn't. But then, neither is the South the South
most of the time. Competing descriptions of the beast abound: there
is the black South and the white South, and that in-between thing of
Jimmy Carter's called The New South, which remains a great idea. The
black South begins in slavery and spirituals, moves through the Mississippi Delta blues into the civil rights movement, forges a great literature, and hovers now in new forms of separatism and strife, a mix
of power and powerlessness. The white South spans the range from the
tobacco-drenched, snake-handling South of Jesse Helms to the bumbling uncertainties of D. Ross McElwee, the protagonist of the 1986
documentary film *Sherman's March*, wandering through his sentimental
history while pretending to look for Southern history.

The cities of the South are very different from one another. San
Antonio and Little Rock, Arkansas, might as well be Cádiz and Gre-
noble. And New Orleans resembles neither one. Oxford, Mississippi,
while not a city ("Oxford Town, Oxford Town!," sings Bob Dylan), is
so imbued with the self-propelled ideas of its importance to the (lit-

erary) South, it might as well be the capital of this mythic region. From architecture to the habits of their citizens, Southern cities differ and diverge. But, from a more distant vantage point, they do share a history that will not let them sleep. This history, like all history, is the memory of the enemy. Which enemy depends on who's talking.

One time, my friend David Brinks, thinking to reassure me that our conversation was candid, not merely polite, said: "Well, at least you're not a Yankee. You're just a Transylvanian in Dixieland."

What David meant, I think, is that Southerners have two ways of speaking: one amongst themselves and the other when the enemy is present. But then so do Transylvanians. In our history, foreign enemies were numerous: Goths, Visigoths, Mongols, Turks, Austrians, Russians. While those people didn't strictly speak our language, they nonetheless understood it, so we developed a manner of speaking that could be heard one way by them and another by us. At its most pristine, this quality was pure: what they heard was exactly the opposite of what we knew it to mean. Oppression does this to language. When white Southerners don't want Yankees to know what they are saying, they talk funny. When black Southerners don't want white Southerners to know what they are saying they talk funny, too. Take the word "bad." In black English it can mean "good." Man, that was b-a-a-d.

What were we, Transylvanians, saying that we didn't want our masters to overhear? Probably things like, they will never find the place where we hid the virgins. Or, can you see how uncivilized these masters really are? How unrefined, uncultured, and graceless? How void of the suffering that alone leads to wisdom? And, finally, we are going to kill them as soon as they fall asleep.

Our enemies evolved over time from foreign to domestic. After the Turks no longer threatened us, we fell into the vicious grips of native rulers who did their work through spies. We became suspicious of one another. Once more, the language of everyday life had to preserve and promote ambiguity, paradox, mystery, and deniability. But, in addition, it had to aid the survival of a private self that drew whatever existence it had from the blanket denial of anything affirmative. (Affirmation being the official credo. For instance, the correct answer to the question asked by the political commissar: "Does God exist or not?" was: "Yes, God does not exist." To which the private self might add: "Not!" in precisely the way teens use it now.)

Such qualities also became the hallmarks of our literature which, more than everyday speech, was beholden to preserving our national identity. But what was easy for oral expression, with its inexhaustible resources of tone, intonation, hesitations, ironies, and silences, was more difficult in writing, which is sadly committed to a kind of permanence.

Our writers, the poets in particular, developed a rich, metaphorical language, fairly throbbing with ambiguity, which gave the censors nightmares and heightened the readers' pleasure in their own cleverness. At the end of the eighties, when communism collapsed in Romania, we had a refined intellectual class composed of clever scribes, super-alert censors, and readers who believed that their savoir faire constituted a sort of revolutionary activity. However, on the same day that communism collapsed, this literature and its readers collapsed as well. Overnight, what had been a shorthand of literary resistance became historical. This momentous collapse was succeeded by an indiscriminate flood of language inspired by American popular culture. The international youth lingo of music, the T-shirt haiku, the scandal-sheet headline, the faux grandeur of pop sociology, psychology, and business—all of these swept over the sensation-starved natives like the spirit seizing the members of First Pentecostal in Araby, Louisiana.

The American Civil War has been over for some time now for the winners. Dave Brinks's hypothetical Yankee has forgotten all about it, and thinks of it as something to be learned in school. But in the South the Civil War—or the War Between the States as they call it in some white places—never ended. Allan Gurganus, the author of *Oldest Living Confederate Widow Tells All*, puts it this way:

> Growing up in the South is really like growing up in ancient Greece. If you see the ruined temples all the time, you have to wonder what the culture was. Northerners don't live with the reality of the war, because they haven't lived with ruins the way we have. The losers always feel the war more than the winners.

Mr. Gurganus's Southerner as noble Greek wandering about the ruins of his grandeur is a well-established cliché of Southern literature, which is as full of funeraria as the cemeteries themselves. We commonly associate Walker Evans with Depression-era pictures of tenant farmers' shacks and country stores with hand-lettered signs, but one of his projects is quite different. Evans took a series of photographs between 1948 and 1952, meant to evoke the landscape of William Faulkner's books. This photographic essay, "Faulkner Country," appeared in *Vogue* magazine in 1948, to coincide with the publication of Faulkner's first novel in six years, *Intruder in the Dust*. This was a Faulkner moment in America. After thirteen books and a number of screenplays, Faulkner was finally acknowledged as one of America's great writers. Evans had long admired Faulkner, as well as other Southern writers, like Thomas Wolfe and Erskine Caldwell, to whose work he was introduced by his friend James Agee. Evans's Faulkner Country consisted of many tombstones, forlorn farm houses, peeling churches, a few decaying mansions, and vast stretches of land. The South Evans portrayed was empty of people but full of ghosts.

Faulkner himself was inspired by the Evans photographs to write a story called "Sepulture South: Gaslight," in which the narrator, a boy, describes what a funeral procession encounters as it approaches the cemetery:

> And now we could already see them, gigantic and white, taller on their marble pedestals than the rose-and-honeysuckle-choked fence, looming into the very trees themselves . . . gazing forever eastward with their empty marble eyes—not symbols: not angels of mercy or winged seraphim or lambs or shepherds, but effigies of the actual people themselves as they had been in life . . . carved in Italian stone by expensive Italian craftsmen and shipped the long costly way by sea back to become one more among the invincible sentinels guarding the temple of our Southern mores. . . .

I don't know about these "Southern mores" or "morae" (Faulkner overdoes maudlin here, and that's a tall order!). But he does tell us that these statues are *white*. For Faulkner, these statues were glyphs of absence. For the contemporary white Southerner, the presence of tombstones is a guarantee of continuity, the surest sign of their *presence*. And it's no mean thing: most of America is so spanking new, its tombstones look as if they come from the Home Depot. Blacks can look to their music, which is still living, and feel both absence and presence. The old black songs are like the old white tombstones, only a lot more portable.

To me, tombstones *and* songs matter. One of the comforts that New Orleans offers a Transylvanian is the enthusiasm of the natives for the dead. It won't do, however, to confuse the tombstones of New Orleans with those described by Faulkner. In fact, they are opposites, being both black and white, stationary and animated. Many of the New Orleans dead are sent to their final places of rest with jazz, libations, and joy. The "funeral ovens" where the dead bake are well cared for, they project an aura of community, they wink at the passersby, they tell their stories without much prompting. New Orleans is Creole, Catholic, cosmopolitan, sinful, and artistic. The emptiness that wafts out of Faulkner's sepulture is thankfully missing here.

New Orleans has the best antebellum houses in America and most of them, surprisingly, are not mausoleums. At the same time, it is not hard to foresee a day when they will be. Already a good number of them have been turned into bed-and-breakfasts that offer the tourist a kitsch version of Southern history replete with Victorian and Edwardian bric-a-brac. This kitsch is itself part of an evolving Southern history—a history full of ironies that still await their writers. Parodies of grandeur are not the only aspects of the new Southern kitsch. You can buy mass-produced mammy dolls in New Orleans. This less-than-benign kitschification is taken to another extreme in a restaurant on Chartres Street called The Slave Exchange. The original building was an actual slave exchange. I wouldn't eat there, but tourists flock there, drawn by what I can only imagine is the thrill of Sepulture without any attending awe.

As recent a phenomenon as Elvis Presley has already been turned inside out by the perverse demands of commerce and inverted pride. Elvis Presley, who pretty much became a parody of himself toward the end of his career, has already gone through two turns of the kitsch wheel. The Elvis cult, which has spawned tons of junk, has now come around to the point where it is hard to separate hokiness from reverential worship.

Much Southern culture now has gone postmodern in a very short time, and without the help of Disney. The noncorporate nature of this postmodernity is the only good thing about it, an homage, you might say, to the persistent inventiveness of the repressed.

Not all is postmodern, however. Some of it is sober retro. In the last decade, a new white religion has sprung up in the South—as if we needed another one: it is called Restoration. While, technically, the name refers only to buildings, it is in fact indicative of an ideology. In its pure form, it is a cult practiced by preservation societies with the tourism bureau behind them. Our restorationists fight valiantly for the accuracy of cornices and original moldings. In its ideological form, the cult of restoration has gained new life from the cultural and political retrogression of our national politics. Mr. Gurganus's noble Greek now comes in any number of white flavors.

Here is a provisional taxonomy of the noble (white) Greek: 1) the tourist, 2) the hick, and 3) the promoter.

1) The tourist comes in two varieties: a) the ironic tourist and b) the plain tourist.

a) The ironic tourist is the hip white tourist. Sometimes he is an aging hipster-gone-North-but-come-back-to-the-roots tourist, who puts black music and primitive religious art on the itinerary. For this type of tourist, authenticity is a must. Authenticity in this case is always black. White Southern culture is both too personal and too painful to observe without the palliative lens of irony.

D. Ross McElwee's *Sherman's March* is an ironic odyssey that "retraces the title Civil War trek while simultaneously examining the mystique of Southern womanhood." The pathos-filled protagonist tours his own life while rambling about Southern ruins. This ironic variety of tourism is made possible only by the awareness of its deeply paradoxical and personal nature. McElwee is on a quest. The conflation of ruins with one's personal life is a fountainhead of Southern literature.

b) The plain white tourist does not have the ironist's postmodern solace. He visits what he believes to be his own past, an exotic place indeed. In the midst of McDonald's-choked highways and one thousand television channels, he becomes a noble Greek for a moment. When he is done touring the mansion, he will go to McDonald's and say the following to his fellow creature-tourist: "We had a civilization here,

Marge." And, depending on how many black people might be listening, he will then proceed to outline the lost virtues of a world in which everybody, master and slave, knew their place and took care of each other accordingly. These lost virtues do not proceed, mind you, from either worthy Southern literature or the physical lessons of the ruins. They proceed from the backward folklore of racism, a mostly oral or pamphlet-driven tradition. The connection from a grand mansion to a system of lost virtues is placed there by a resurgent ideology.

This type of architectural-sentimental tourist has been noted. Hal Crowther in his essay, "Eating Rats at Vicksburg," tells a story the novelist Jill McCorkle, a white North Carolinian, told him: "about a woman who was fawning over the Civil War historian Shelby Foote at a writers' conference. 'Oh, don't you just wish you'd been alive back in those days?' the woman gushed directly at a black writer, Tina McElroy Ansa, who answered simply, 'No.' "

Now, what I like about this story is not just the sublime simple-mindedness of the question but its intricate context. It's a story told by one writer to another about another writer whose presence facilitates an exchange between a tourist and yet another writer. That's four writers for one tourist, a ratio that is possible only in the context of a Southern literary conference.

Let us now turn to the other types of noble Greeks:

2) The hick (*aussi blanc*) drives a pickup with Confederate flag decals and is in open rebellion against the values of the United States. He is ready to fight the Civil War all over again and is doing so as we speak. Elvis Presley has somehow gotten mixed up in the glories of the Confederacy. One is never sure if Richmond, Virginia, or Memphis's Graceland is the true Mecca. The Confederate flag flies (symbolically and literally) over both.

My good friend Vernon Chadwick had the outlandish idea of saving the Confederate flag by psychedelicizing it, making it hip. His slogan, above an electrically colored rebel flag, was "Make It Funky." Vernon's concept was, I think, to defuse (or infuse) the object by incorporating Elvis Presley, Delta blues, rock 'n' roll, and pond-raised catfish, in other words, those things that most Americans consider most American. In other words yet, he wanted to conflate those national Southern treasures with other, not so treasured, aspects that are currently represented by the cult of ruins, the religion of restoration. Unfortunately, in back of this seemingly postmodern mélange, legions of demons lie in wait, chief among which is racism. The Confederate flag is wholly unironic to the racist. For American Nazis, the Klan, and the Christian Reich, the Confederate flag stands for white supremacy. What they miss about the Old South is slavery. And that's what they see in the Confederate flag.

The third type of noble Greek is 3) the promoter. Nostalgia is good business in the South now. While it makes perfect economic sense for New Orleans and other decaying cities, the profession involves the faking of history through boosterism. Here is an example: I wrote an article for *Playboy* magazine about the quite extraordinary crimes committed over the past four years by the New Orleans police (herein incorporated in the section on New Orleans). The sordid story of our cops had already come out in bits and pieces and gotten plenty of national attention. All I did was to string together some of the more spectacular incidents in narrative form. The head of the local chamber of commerce called before the magazine was even out—how he'd gotten word of it is a mystery to me—and told me that both the mayor and the governor were mad at me. "You gave the city a black eye," he said. Now, I only type with one finger. Think what I could do with ten. In any case, at the same time *Playboy* came out, *Guest Informant* also came out with my lead article on the glories, history, food, et al of New Orleans. *Guest Informant* can be found in every hotel room in New Orleans and is most tourists' first literature on the city. Is there a contradiction? No. But boosterism, which overstates the genuine delights of the place, suffers exaggerated pain from criticism. Among other neuroses of the South, there is an inferiority complex or, let's call it, a sensitivity to the views of outsiders.

A Transylvanian in Dixieland, provided that he is not a Yankee, has no choice but to feel at home among the many forms of alienation that flourish here. Alienation is not a uniform state, the same in Jean-Paul Sartre as in Anne Rice. It's not only not uniform but it comes in a great many varieties. Walker Percy, recalling the genesis of his novel *The Moviegoer*, puts it this way:

> I remember we were renting a little shotgun cottage in New Orleans, and I was sitting on the back porch there one day, and I was thinking, why not take a young man who was alienated in a peculiarly American way—not like a dogmatic French alienation, but in a special Southern, New Orleans way—and set him down in Gentilly, a middle-class section of New Orleans? And there I had Binx Bolling in *The Moviegoer*.

Another form of alienation I share with Southerners is an accent. When my friend Dave Brinks was granting that I was not a Yankee he was giving me membership in the "accent club." He didn't as much fear what a Yankee might overhear or how he might misinterpret what he overheard, but simply the physical fact of his accent. A Southern accent used to carry certain assumptions, among them, the suspicion that a fascist hick might be lurking under it. But Southern accents have become quite fashionable these days, to the point where movie actors who'd had them wiped out by voice coaches, are relearning them for movie parts. No such rich history attends my accent. I have no idea what people assume when they hear a Romanian accent. But in these days of xenophobia I wouldn't be surprised if someone might assume that I was stealing his job. I *am* stealing someone's job, only I'm not sure what the job is or who the *someone* is, for that matter.

Alienated accent-bearers hold in common the faculty of fabulation or "the telling of tall tales." Both Southerners and Transylvanians are very good at this. The art of telling a story depends on two things: time to tell it and a childhood spent listening to grown-ups tell stories. Both of these commodities are fast disappearing. Time to tell the story is scarce not only because we have grown busier, but because the stories the media tells us compete for attention and they spare no low trick to get it. A childhood spent listening to grown-ups is no longer available because grown-ups are no longer available, absorbed as they are in listening to the mechanical stories of media programming. The childhood in question is a rural childhood, a childhood available to almost no one after 1940. Back then, to hear Harry Crews tell it:

> Since where we lived and how we lived was almost hermetically sealed from everything and everybody else, fabrication became a way of life. Making up stories, it seems to me now, was not only a way to understand the way we lived but also a defense against it.

Harry Crews goes on to remember his friendship with a black boy and the abrupt end of that friendship. The storytelling and the defenses it put against the real world proved to be no longer sufficient after a certain age. This reminiscence hints at another secret of Southern storytelling. Much of the South's most vital literature today is written by black writers. But even four decades ago, many of the best white Southern writers, Faulkner included, were raised by black mammies. Albert Murray, in his "South to a Very Old Place," quotes Faulkner's elegy to his mammy, then notes: "Many white Southerners go around talking about white womanhood or really about white girlhood which is to say belle-hood, but the conception of *Motherhood*, for some reason almost always comes out *black!*" If language is absorbed with mother's milk, then the storytelling genius of much Southern literature is black.

The tortured intimacy in which blacks and whites lived—and still live—in the South, is mirrored in the complex and tortured relationships within Southern families. The life of Southern fiction flows from these two sources: the family, which is fast disappearing under a river of psychobabble in America, and racial coexistence. As far back as the South doesn't really care to remember, the farrago was there. Here is America's first celebrated observer, Alexis de Tocqueville, in *Democracy in America*:

> I happened to meet an old man, in the South of the Union, who had lived in illicit intercourse with one of his Negresses and had had several children by her, who were born the slaves of their father. He had, indeed, frequently thought of bequeathing to them at least their liberty; but years elapsed before he could surmount the legal obstacles to their emancipation, and meanwhile his old age had come and he was about to die. He pictured to himself his sons dragged from market to market and passing from the authority of a parent to the rod of the stranger, until these horrid anticipations worked his expiring imagination into frenzy. When I saw him, he was prey to all the anguish of despair; and I then understood how awful is the retribution of Nature upon those who have broken her laws.

The South in its passions, faux passions, nostalgias, faux nostalgias, and complexes of various sorts, is the throbbing matrix of the great American dilemma of race. The best line of poetry ever written describes this situation, as well as many others. It is by bluesman Robert Johnson. He sings: "You're closer to me, baby, than Jesus to the cross!"

Oxford, Mississippi

Oxford Town, the newspaper that subtitles itself "a journal of civilization," asked a number of its citizens, "What do you see when you think of Oxford?" All five folk surveyed named street corners or stores. Most significant, perhaps, of all the answers was Peyton Hooper's, who said: "Van Buren Avenue and South Fifth Street because the oldest people I ever knew in Oxford spent their whole lives on that one block." Now, to the connoisseur that's as rich a sentence as any ever uttered about the town. It exudes the essence. It carries also a deeper flavor than the sign, OXFORD, A NICE PLACE TO LIVE, which greets the visitor.

I, who am no connoisseur, but merely a visitor, found it surprising that none of the surveyed mentioned what most of the world sees when it thinks of Oxford, namely, its writers. The most famous, of course, is William Faulkner, whose mansion at Rowan Oak is a museum run by the University of Mississippi. Oxford is so imbued with the mystique of Faulkner it is hard to imagine how other writers might thrive here, but they do. There is Barry Hannah, whose stories draw surreal strength from the same Mississippi mud. There is Larry Brown, an ex-fireman, whose memories of fires have sparked national interest. And then, there is John Grisham, the lawyer turned mystery novelist, whose treeless hilltop mansion stands over Route 6 awaiting the arrival of full-grown trees to shield it from gawking motorists. Grisham has also built a baseball field on his grounds, for use by his son's little league team, an extravagance that has old Oxfordans gritting their eyeteeth in disapproval. Nouveau riche is not quite as bad as "carpetbagger," but you can *hear* the proximity in that gritting. In reply to all that, or perhaps in deference to all that, Grisham has sponsored *The Oxford American*, an outstanding quarterly magazine that's had its finger on the erratic pulse of the South since the first issue.

Hannah, Brown, and Grisham are among the town's best-known literati, but chances are the vague-looking young Republicans circling the town square are all would-be writers. This is no bohemia, to be sure, and the scene that Oxford offers or gropes for is the very opposite of bohemia: scandals are well wrapped, not flaunted, drinking is done at home, and philandering in the fields. What interests writers here is the layers of respectability under which may be found as seamy an America as ever graced Greenwich Village. Some of them might argue that the upholding of respectability, family, church, and proper manners *despite* the heat-induced lassitude is the high calling of their Art. (The deeper South one goes, both in space and time, the more majuscules appear, like funnel clouds in the sepulchral skies.) Being small, Oxford has the distinction of being a perfect laboratory. But it's not for outsiders: you have to be born here. Otherwise, it makes no sense. Outsiders do come and are made very welcome in the classic fried-catfish style of Southern hospitality. The people are, as they say, warm. Like the weather. And sultry, moody, and deep like it, too.

Following in the steps of Alice Walker, Ellen Douglas, and Rick Bass, all writers who had recently read from their work at Square Books in Oxford, I arrived on a sweltering late summer day to add my two cents to the town's literary piggy bank. My host, Vernon Chadwick, the publisher of *The Southern Reader*, was out to make sure that I was treated better than your average visitor. He likes my work. Vernon talked his sister, Mrs. Patricia Lamar, into putting me up in her guest house.

The Lamar homestead was on the other side of the road from Rowan Oak, Mr. Faulkner's mansion. Pat Lamar, a former Miss Mississippi, was a city councilmember. Her husband, Dr. Lamar, was of distinguished Oxford stock: the main street in Oxford is called Lamar Boulevard. Mrs. Lamar had recently run for mayor, but had been defeated by scandal: her enemies had insinuated that she'd had her grounds mowed at the same time as Mr. Faulkner's, at taxpayers' expense. (She was eventually elected mayor in 1996.)

Indeed, the Lamars' grounds were manicured to that perfection possible only through the use of oligarchic gardeners. Pat Lamar, in middle age, was still quite beautiful. She showed me the cedarwood guest cabana where I was going to stay, and then asked if I would care for a tour of the main house, a lovely mansion on the other side of a sparkling swimming pool. Trailed by a less than enthusiastic Dr. Lamar, Pat led the way, explaining with passion the authentic features of the construction.

Mrs. Lamar treated me to brief histories of her collections of prints, furniture, and paintings, and introduced the oil portraits of stalwart Mississippians who'd fought many a good fight. (And lost.) I remarked on what surely was a timely and costly hobby. "Oh, we are junkers, you know," smiled Mrs. Lamar toward Dr. Lamar, a joke that wasn't so much meant to show modesty but duration. It was a bond between them. The mansion was so resplendent there was really very little room for messes.

At one point, we were standing in the finely appointed room of their son, Lucius, whose photographs beamed from above the quilted bed, piled high with embroidered pillows. Lucius was a handsome devil at all ages, smiling an insouciant Oscar Wildeish smile at every photo op. Mrs. Lamar hurried through this room, but the hitherto taciturn Dr. Lamar intervened: "Show them Lucius's closet, dear!"

There was but the sliver of an icy millisecond. "Oh, why in the world would we want to do that?" Mrs. Lamar never broke the beautiful smile on her pleasing countenance.

Dr. Lamar insisted. Mrs. Lamar shrugged, and shook her perfect hair a little. "Men . . . and their closets!" She pulled the baroque latch of a beautiful lacquered closet door, and I saw, piled densely inside, hundreds, maybe *thousands* of mammy dolls! Going deep into the recesses of what appeared to be an endless closet, were the skirt-smothered forms of plump black women with huge eyes, their kindly faces staring out at us.

"Lucius started collecting them in third grade," explained Dr. Lamar, utterly pleased by my badly concealed surprise.

Scions of Southern families are raised by black women to this day. For an instant I thought I saw the intricate workings of a Southern history as deep as Lucius's closet. Mrs. Lamar shut the door softly, not pleased with Dr. Lamar's cruelty. He was going to pay for this.

Later, when we strolled past the sumptuous kitchen I glimpsed what appeared to be Dr. Lamar's allotted area of the house, a place as messy and manly as the house was spotless and feminine. Dr. Lamar's area was restricted to a pool table and a pipe stand. When we approached his zone he growled a warning. We retreated, and visited instead a sumptous office chock full of hunting trophies. This was Dr. Lamar's official den, where his proper double resided.

Later, reclining on the luxurious sage-scented pillows in my little Ralph Lauren cottage, I tried to sort out my impressions: I had participated in a High Mass of Restoration, the South's new religion, while being instructed, with broad hints, that the personal was the historical where the persons concerned were indeed Persons of Import. This sort of thinking, spoken with an accent, was aided immeasurably by the guest house itself, which sported what a Ralph Lauren imitation never could: portraits of *real* ancestors.

Refreshed by my insights, I thought to enjoy the azure pool for a quick dip. But no sooner did I step outside than a gaggle of accordion-pleated beasts with bare fangs hurled itself at me, forcing me back into the house. These creatures, I learned from Vernon, who rescued me about an hour later, were a species of dogs called shar-pei, which had been bred by Chinese emperors to patrol the perimeters of their palaces. They were fierce guardians of the square enclosing the castle and were ready at all times to kill anyone who overstepped.

Vernon made sure that my impressions of the town followed a rigorous and gradual course that would reveal both its pleasures and its ambiguities. After he rescued me from the shar-peis, we walked to the Square, the heart of Oxford, toward the courthouse, a building familiar to anyone who has read Faulkner. Standing in front of it is a tall column atop which a Confederate soldier leans on his rifle. This is the Confederate Monument on the Square, erected by the United Daughters of the Confederacy in 1907. Vernon, who was wearing a T-shirt sporting a green Confederate flag with the legend, "Make It Funky," pointed out a tree to the left of the courthouse where a man was lynched and hung in 1908. This incident had, of course, a literary echo in Faulkner.

Thus edified, I followed Vernon to Square Books, the locus of my upcoming recital, and the quarters of its affable proprietors Richard and Lisa Howorth. If the New South exists and is not merely the fiction of a grinning Georgia peanut farmer, it might be embodied by this couple. Richard was of old Oxford stock too, but he'd brought the world here and was quite outspoken about the town's secrets.

Square Books is remarkable: its two floors display excellent selections, with an understandable bias toward Southern writers. The well-stocked magazine selection would not be out of place in Cambridge, Massachusetts, or New York City, and one could easily imagine the Old South descending with pitchforks to torch the place for some of its heathen contents. But history *vincit omnia*. The pitchforks are in the museum, though the urge to torch things is still quite active, as evidenced by the burning of black churches all over the South.

The books most prominently displayed carried little cards with the employees' brief reviews and recommendations. The employees, like bookstore clerks everywhere, were, of course, incredibly hip. They recommended no popular reads: their selections thumbed their postmodern noses at the would-be hick if one dared come in. Upstairs, a small café was busy fortifying the customers for marathon browsing. My audience, sizable but not excessive, was polite and suspicious. After the reading, the questioning aimed to establish my Southern credentials or, at least, review my application for them:

"What do you think of New York?" asked a ragged fellow who, obviously, did not think much of it.

"Fine place to be young and rich in," I said. That could have been an insult. It might have implied that Oxford, by comparison, was for the poor and the aged. An astute Southern literatus might have caught it. But my interviewer didn't. He seemed satisfied. He had stated his view.

"What do you think of the Confederate flag?" asked another man, an intense look under furrowed brows. He gave the impression that this, to him, was a matter of extreme importance. I, who have used the official currency of the state as toilet paper on occasion, felt quickly challenged.

"Well," I said, "the swastika is a traditional Native American motif, but I don't see that we should fly it from the courthouse roof."

That didn't go over too well. That was putting too much juice into history. It's one thing to pour passion into correct cornices and period doorknobs, another to touch the still undressed wounds of Southern pride. For a moment, I was sure that a challenge was forthcoming. I am no gentleman, though. I looked to Vernon for strength. He was smiling widely, as if to say: "This is what we brought this fiery, controversial Transylvanian here for!"

"What do *you* think of it?" I asked my audience, collectively.

"We like it all," said a young man clad in international hipster black, "the flag, the blues, the heat, the stupids, the whiskey, and the Faulkner House. . . ."

Everyone laughed, because the truth of that assertion was self-evident to the younger white Southerners. They were intrigued, and possibly proud of their whole history. They were enthralled equally by lynching and by the blues. They had an equal-opportunity view of the past that eliminated controversy by embracing and subsuming all realities under the sentimental banner of history. Our history, love it or leave it.

(Not as confident as the young, the chancellor at the University of Mississippi hired a New York (!) public relations firm to evaluate Mississippi's historical symbols. The chancellor's action stirred such passion in the breasts of local patriots, it was proposed that the man himself be rendered historical pronto.)

Despite my pugnaciousness, the discussion went on afterward at Proud Larry's, a fine café and bar next door. Everything in the informal conversation bespoke a passion for letters and, not surprisingly, there were literary factions. Vernon, for instance, didn't think much of *The Oxford Review*, John Grisham's ambitious journal. His own *Southern Reader* was engaged in a polemic with the nearly universal flattery of this new publication. From the pages of *Oxford Town* I gleaned the editors' unbridled contempt for literary tourism, as typified for them by the sign FAULKNER ALLEY, which had been pasted over an alley in the Square by the evil forces of development and tourism. This alley had, apparently, served Mr. Faulkner as a shortcut between Rowan Oak and the bars on the Square, a shortcut necessitated by his unsteady gait after the consumption of large quantities of bourbon. The sight of the great writer, supported by his wife, Estelle, both of them clinging carefully to the sidewalk on their way home, is still vivid in the memories of some old residents.

My education continued later in the day with a walk to Rowan Oak itself. Along the route, I learned the history of various houses that figured in Faulkner's life and fiction. There was the Elma Meek House at 803 University Avenue, Faulkner's first home after he married Estelle Oldham in 1929. The writer spent afternoons writing at a table in the garden, and looking over at a dilapidated mansion that became the setting of his creepy tale, "A Rose for Emily." Emily, you may recall, poisoned the Northern cad who had seduced her, and then slept with the body for the next forty years.

I could believe it. The unfolding of literary details was the very process by which Faulkner's fiction had built the town of Oxford and then the South itself. The construct of literal worlds from literature is by no means new. Hannibal, Missouri, is a town constructed by Mark Twain, that persona constructed by Samuel Clemens. The country of Macondo is in reality Colombia. It is the fictional country of Gabriel García Márquez, who modeled it on Faulkner's Yoknapatawpha County, where Oxford is. But there is something more about Faulkner's South, namely the meeting of a region violently bereft of identity with the myths of a writer. The South soaked up Faulkner and continues to sop up its writers' fictions like a big, thirsty blotter.

The shimmering heat that made everything slightly indistinct and surreal held more than a hint of madness and excessive abandon. The houses themselves exuded distinct personalities, simultaneously mysterious and hostile, open and welcoming. It was as if it had now fallen to them, in all their hybrid intimate detail, to defend the unspoken truth against the intrusions of men with typewriters, no matter how astute. Vernon knew many of these houses' stories intimately, since he had helped restore some of them, and he was related to almost everyone living in a *truly* historic house. Of pretenders, of course, there was no end, Vernon warned me, holding as a shining example John Grisham's nouveau monstrosity on the hill.

We stopped by the home of one of Vernon's uncles who was not there. We were bid welcome anyway by the cook. The cook, a not-so-young-anymore shirtless man had the hungover look of someone as intimately conversant with bourbon as Mr. Faulkner. He dragged himself ahead of us, pointing to cases full of historical objects, but clearly his interest was flagging. The pipe of Jeff Davis, president of the Confederacy, might as well have been corncob. Aspirins were of greater immediate concern. Now, I would pass over the delicate matter of *cooks*, but literature does have its indelicate requirements.

We passed by Mrs. Lamar's again and this time I met her son, Lucius. Having seen his doll collection, I felt wickedly in the know. Lucius was as perfect a specimen of young Southern aristocracy as it is possible to encounter *without* falling into literature. He was extremely handsome, in a curly-haired Bacchus mode. His conversation was sprinkled with expensive cars and memories of wild times in glamorous places. He was evidently aware of his pedigree, having been named after his great-grandfather, Lucius Quintus Cincinnatus Lamar, the first associate supreme court justice from Mississippi. Lurking behind his witty repartee, like busts in a gallery, were the figures of illustrious Mississippians.

Lucius took us on the tour of Rowan Oak and Bailey's Woods,

his childhood playground. The bucolic verses of lesser English poets bounced about my skull as we sauntered over the immaculate lawns toward the writer's colonnaded abode.

William Faulkner bought this antebellum house in 1930 for $6,000 and spent considerable time restoring it. The rows of cedars leading to the house, the brick walkways, and the gardens all bore the writer's personal touch. The house stood expectantly, in a state of writerly readiness. We peered through a window at Mr. Faulkner's typewriter, which gets dusted every day.

Behind the house were the tangled shades of Bailey's Woods, where the writer liked to go riding, and where Lucius, age fourteen, burned his leg one summer day with some ointment from a can he found while playing here. It was immediately surmised that this can was full of the stuff Mr. Faulkner used to make his horses jump. The writer, who had been notoriously unfriendly to trespassers, did not stop, apparently, even after his death. Lucius showed us his scar, a badge of honor, Mr. Faulkner's signature, in fact.

Bailey's Woods took us into the University Woods over an old railroad bridge. Below us, the old rails were covered by kudzu, a voracious and surreal plant that has turned most of the South into Bosch-like topiary. Vernon explained that Ole Miss students at the start of the century arrived by railroad and passed through a ritual gate into the campus. The many still-extant rituals, much beloved by college men from the South, were, according to Vernon, a kind of link to their noble predecessors in England. And that is how the Middle Ages got to the South. History. And then came kudzu, impressionist and ubiquitous like postmodernism.

We passed this abandoned-looking gate, and emerged into the Grove, another ceremonial site on the Ole Miss campus. Here, Vernon professed with evident emotion, one of Mississippi's most sacrosanct rituals took place every year, namely the Twirling Contest. Girls from all over the South twirled competitively in the Grove. From here also, Ole Miss's football team, the Rebels, spurred to a froth by the skilled twirling, went forth in godlike splendor to the stadium.

"There is nothing like the sound of the brass band playing 'Dixie' on an early fall afternoon while the entire town is having a tailgate party!" proclaimed my host.

Well, maybe. The white columns of the University of Mississippi's oldest building, the Lyceum, looked familiar. I had seen the famous news photo. This is where Ross Barnett, the governor of Mississippi in 1963, had stood with his arms crossed to bar the way as two federal marshals escorted James Meredith, the first black student to desegregate the all-white university. "Which one of you gentlemen is James Meredith?" Ross Barnett is said to have demanded of the two white marshals and the one black young man. Ole Miss is now desegregated, but Mississippi hasn't forgotten Ross Barnett: on the road from Oxford to Jackson there are signs for the ROSS BARNETT RESERVOIR and the ROSS BARNETT LAKE.

Oxford may be a writers' fiction, but the surrounding area is rural Mississippi, the delta that gave birth to the blues. This is where Robert Johnson, Muddy Waters, and Howlin' Wolf hailed from. Highway 61, "the Delta's main street," runs like a rambling blues through the nearby towns of Rolling Fork, Anguilla, Alligator, and Clarksdale.

I almost expected to hear one of the great bluesmen later that night when Vernon and Lucius took me to Taylor's in Taylor, Mississippi, just outside of Oxford, for catfish. The restaurant was located inside an old grocery store and the smell of frying catfish was thick enough to cling to my clothes for days. But the catfish came whole, and there were several of them on a plate, atop a mound of french fries, flanked by homemade coleslaw. The walls at Taylor's were covered by thousands of autographs left there over the years by Ole Miss students. I left mine too, on the frame of the door, just above the scrawl of a '69 sophomore.

It was midnight when we stumbled out of Taylor's, stuffed and sweaty, but the night wasn't over. Not by far. Driving fast on the familiar road, Vernon drove to "Graceland Two," a modest house in Holly Springs, Mississippi, that had little to distinguish it from the sleepy country homes surrounding it. Nothing but the fact that it was open twenty-four hours and it was a shrine to Elvis Presley.

The keepers of the flame were Paul MacLeod and his son, Elvis Aaron Presley MacLeod. Both of them looked like Presley, the earlier and the later version. The house was crammed full of Elvis memorabilia, including every issue of *TV Guide* in which the King was mentioned since the day of his death. The MacLeods threw open their treasure trove and proceeded to spin fantastic tales of Elvis. The elder MacElvis had spent the night with Elvis's body at the mortuary. His wife left him shortly thereafter when, given a choice between her and Elvis, MacLeod chose Elvis. We went from room to room, turning over sacred shreds of King-infused materials. In one room upstairs, an old woman was snoring in a bed surrounded by mounds of holy clippings. We tiptoed around the woman, who was the elder MacElvis's mom and the younger's grandma, and tracked back downstairs for more mourning. This would have gone on, I'm sure, until dawn, if I had not made to leave. The worship-heavy air of the heavily draped house was oppressive in precisely the same way the real Elvis's rooms at Graceland One were. All Elvises suffered from fear of fresh air and loved the vampiric air of the crypt. The sadness of the South has this Gothic branch that goes through Faulkner as well as Elvis. And by extension, through Oxford and the Elvi.

Vernon is an Elvis scholar at the University of Mississippi and the organizer of the yearly Elvis Conference, which had originally taken place in Oxford, but had been moved to Memphis after the university brass (which hired New York PR men to evaluate the South!) had protested the appearance of a lesbian Elvis impersonator at the yearly event. Vernon had often brought his students to spend the night at Graceland Two. At that time, the elder McLeod's wife still lived in the house, so the students had to put up with her proprietary grumbling as they spread their casual bedrolls among the legendary artifacts.

Graceland Two stands halfway between Elvis's birthplace in Tupelo, Mississippi, and Graceland in Memphis. Close by is the store where Elvis is said to have purchased his first guitar. Lucius told me Elvis hadn't been sure whether he wanted a guitar or a gun. In any case, he didn't have enough money for either, so the store owner said he'd lend him the money if he bought the guitar. Just think: he might have been a two-bit hood instead of King. History.

Next day at Mrs. Lamar's guest house, I was slapped awake by the brutal light that came through the velvet fringes of the curtains. I squinted at the outside and saw the azure swimming pool glittering invitingly in its shar-pei-patrolled loneliness. I'd had a cavalcade of dreams led, it seems, by a barefoot cook who was determined to get me to some place called "the pinnacle of civilization." I don't think I got there because a huge guitar-playing catfish barred the way. The pool looked good enough to cleanse me of the bits of dream still clinging to my tenuous person. However, the thought that several of the ugliest creatures ever devised by selective breeding would hurl themselves at me stayed my progress. These wrinkled, accordion-like beasts with bared teeth, were exercising the class privileges of their owners without the niceties of literature. Anything that stepped either in or out of the designated class structure activated them for destruction. More history. The history of China, but still.

If the reporter from *Oxford Town* was to ask me now what it was that I see when I think of Oxford, I'd say: "Faulkner Elvis Catfish Shar-pei Twirling Kudzu," pronounced as a single word. Of course, there is more to it, especially more history, but I'm afraid that Disney is already working on it. As are scores of writers in Oxford proper. When Hollywood remade the South in *Gone With the Wind*, they missed a few spots. Oxford is one of them.

An Afternoon in Little Rock

They say that the mountain will come to Muhammad if he stands still long enough, and that's exactly what happened to Little Rock when Bill Clinton became president. The big world, which had pretty much ignored the quiet little town in the heart of Arkansas, came calling with a bang. It shook up the regular folks, startled the local restaurateurs, electrified the hoteliers, turned on the entrepreneurs, set the T-shirt and button makers ablaze, and turned the ink wretches at the *Arkansas Democrat-Gazette* into book writers. It happened fast, it was exciting, and it was a typical American story about what happens when business as usual becomes everybody's business. It was also another moment of glory for the South, which has owned the presidency since Lyndon Johnson. That is, if you are willing to consider Texas and Southern California as part of the South, which psychologically they (somewhat) are.

I came calling on downtown Little Rock six months after Clinton's first-term victory, curious about the milieu our youngest president since John Kennedy had been hatched in. Bill Clinton had used his small-town, small-state roots to great advantage during the campaign. The

Rhodes scholar was all but forgotten while the Good Ol' Boy did his just-folks thing.

It was a Saturday in mid-February, and Little Rock was as sleepy as Juarez at siesta time. I met Philip and Karen Martin for lunch at the Capitol Hotel, a splendid old establishment that is the local watering hole for journalists. Established in 1877, it has a grand marble staircase, marble columns, and a long bar from which the local pundits have watched the scene for over a century. But when Bill Clinton won the Democratic nomination, the world press took over the Capitol Hotel and kept the locals out. On this lazy afternoon, we were just about alone in the bar. Philip and Karen both work at the *Arkansas Democrat-Gazette*, which used to be the *Arkansas Democrat* and is now the only paper in town after the much-lamented *Arkansas Gazette* shut down.

The *Gazette*, founded in 1819 by William Woodruff, had been the oldest paper west of the Mississippi. Karen, who worked for it, was still nostalgic. The employees had held candlelight vigils when the paper shut down. Shortly after that, it became the local campaign headquarters for Clinton. "The *Gazette* shut down so quickly," Karen explained, "Clinton's staff kept finding our files and things."

After the storm that came with the Clinton presidential campaign, Little Rock had a brief respite. The locals gathered their wits about them, retook possession of their haunts, and started writing books. Then Whitewater came. Suddenly, the ascendance of local politics to the national level took on deeper resonance. Philip coauthored a book on Hillary Clinton (with Rex Nelson) and prefaced one on Bill Clinton by David Gallen, though he'd once sworn that he wouldn't write a book about either one of them. Everyone then started writing a book about the Clintons. Scores of people turned out to have been the first couple's good friends. Philip claims no such thing. "I never smoked pot with Bill or got into a hot tub with them." But they were acquainted.

Well, it's a small town. If I'd been living here, I would have known them too. And so, the thought of living here crossed my mind. What would it be like to live here in Little Rock instead of the fabulous night capital of music, food, and crime?

"You'd love it," Karen said. "You'll see."

The tuna salad arrived, two major lumps of tuna on half tomato slices, with assorted fruit wedges. It was good, in an old-fashioned way. It was like the fifties—peaceful, safe, bland, comforting. It was straight out of a cookbook called *Thirty Years at the Mansion*, which collects the recipes best loved by Arkansas governors. It had been favored by several. The others had equally mainstream tastes. Governor Orval E. Faubus, for instance, who was famous for calling in the National Guard to keep desegregation from being implemented, liked "Old-Fashioned Pie," "Chicken Casserole," and something called "Exotic Turkey Salad," in which the exotic part was provided by a can of pineapple chunks "with juice." His successor, Winthrop Rockefeller, who was famous for completely renovating the decrepit Governor's Mansion, was the gourmand of the bunch. He feasted on such things as "Lobster Newburg," "Broccoli Soufflé," and "Vichyssoise." This invasion of haute cuisine didn't last long. Governor Dale Bumpers took things firmly back to country-solid "Buttermilk Chicken" and "Stuffed Pork Chops." He was followed by Governor David Pryor's "Broccoli Casserole," which led directly to Bill Clinton's "Chicken and Rice," "Cold Steak Salad," and "Jello Pineapple Seven-Up Salad." No wonder eating out at McDonald's became such a dining experience for the future president.

But don't be fooled. The wave of gourmandise sweeping the Union had reached Little Rock. "The best restaurant in town is Alouette, under Chef Dennis Sayer," Karen told me, "now that Chef Andre's been murdered."

Alouette, explained my hosts, was a Swiss-French restaurant, and so was Andre's. Little Rock had, for some reason, experienced an invasion of Swiss chefs in the nineties. Karen remembered nostalgically the first of these, a place called Jacques and Susanne's, where Swiss chefs from all over the world (not just Switzerland; most Swiss chefs live in Brazil) came to train and have fun. Jacques and Susanne's was gone now but a sprinkling of Swiss chefs stayed behind. The doomed Andre had been the best loved, but even though he had been murdered, Swiss cuisine marched on in Little Rock.

Out the window of the Capitol Hotel bar I watched a baffled conventioneer scan the street both ways for some action. He was standing in front of the new convention center and Excelsior Hotel, hoping to catch a whiff of excitement. There wasn't any. He'd missed it by one day. Fifteen thousand deliriously happy people had marched through downtown the day before, celebrating the victory of the Razorbacks in the NCAA basketball championships. At the same time, Operation Rescue, which champions unborn babies, had been picketing the Rose Law Firm for some unfathomable reason. The best way Philip could explain it was that Operation Rescue's founder Randall Terry "wanted to be President so he was starting early by attacking Hillary, who used to work for the Rose Law Firm." The two rallies had mixed, but the sports fans had, thankfully, outnumbered the Christian fundamentalists. The public displays had sapped the energies of the natives.

No wonder they were staying indoors. Downtown Little Rock slumbered like a mountain man with a hangover. The lone tourist, framed by the even lonelier deserted office buildings, looked like Eliot's straw man. I felt for him. I remembered how many times I'd gone in futile search for signs of life in a middle-sized American city, only to end up standing at some bus stop, looking stupid and feeling foolish. "You should have been here yesterday," I was invariably told. "We had the Columbus Day Parade with two thousand topless DARs." (Or so I invariably heard.)

After lunch, we went for a walk on the empty streets. The tallest building in town was the TCBY (The Country's Best Yogurt) Tower, a modest high-rise that had the distinction of having once counted Hillary Rodham Clinton on its corporate board. It wasn't much as buildings go, but there was something comforting about the idea that yogurt had the mightiest house in Little Rock. It made up for the emptiness somehow. And if you counted those Swiss cooks, everything was almost reassuring. This was Small Town, USA, in majuscules.

Arkansas's richest man, the then recently departed Sam Walton, the founder of Wal-Mart, projected the same kind of comforting feeling. Sure, he was also the wealthiest man in the world, but there was something essentially solid, good, old-fashioned, and unpretentious about his fortune. There was no Texas-style melodrama attached to its origin. And that's good, because if Arkansans dislike anything more than pretention, it's Texans.

Philip sniffed contemptuously when I mentioned Dallas, by way of an example of a city that was all buildings and no life. "The place is nothing but snobbery," he intoned. "You need a million just to get invited to a society lunch. In Little Rock, if you donate a thousand dollars to the museum and bring the potato salad, you're high society." I got the impression that the rise of Bill Clinton to the highest office in the land was as much revenge on Texans as it was Arkansan pride. Philip loved his city. He'd left, come back, left again, come back. His explanations varied, but they boiled down to this chamber of commerce formula: it was city living with a country feel:

It's small enough so that people know each other. QED: everybody knows the First Couple. Old-fashioned Southern courtesy is still alive. Crime is low. Housing is relatively inexpensive. In ten minutes' drive you can be in a beautiful spot in the mountains, looking on wide valleys, lying down in wildflower meadows, swimming in clean lakes. You can paddle down the Buffalo River and catch trout. You'd love it here.

Little Rock stands at the meeting place of the Ozarks with the flat plains, in the foothills of the Ouachita Mountains. The air was subtly redolent of mountain flowers. We walked by the Arkansas River, which flowed broad-beamed through town, dividing South from North Little Rock. Wrought-iron bridges arced over the water. Barges hugged the banks.

There *was* a peaceful feeling of well-being here, even without the people. After all, it was Saturday, and in a nice town the family is either at home, cooking and playing basketball, or going for a drive into the country. A long train, car after car filled with redwood chips, passed over the river embankment. The sun was still high in a crisp blue sky. I believed for a moment that I was seeing the soul of the city. Sure, I could live here, the guilty megalopolitan in me said.

We strolled over to the old State House, which was a museum. The old State Capitol bore the date 1836 on the iron gate. It had been in use from 1836 to 1919, which barring recent events, was the time when most of Arkansas's dramatic history took place: the Civil War, its aftermath, Prohibition. It was a handsome structure, housing broad-stroke displays of Arkansas history and prehistory, including a hunting diorama peopled by frightening trappers lugging fresh skins. It didn't seem that Arkansans had spent much time between the log cabin and the space age. No long decadent bourgeois culture to dull their senses.

The museum shop was bursting with Clinton memorabilia. There were blue and white Clinton earrings, perfect for that nostalgia party, campaign buttons, and, best of all, a postcard of Bill's first-grade class at Brockwood Elementary School in Hope, Arkansas. One of the goofy-looking tykes with funny hair was Mack McLarty, who became the president's chief of staff. Who said that first-grade friendships didn't last?

The youngish woman behind the museum-shop counter tried to interest me in a first-day cancellation of a Bill Clinton postcard. I told her that I was a writer not a collector. Well, she was, it turned out, a writer, too. She was only working here until her novel sold. Now there were four of us writers in the old Arkansas State House, and no one at all, except for one baffled tourist, on the streets. I asked her if there were many writers in Little Rock. "Sure," she said, "they are like actors in Hollywood."

I tried to imagine. Writers everywhere, wearing their coonskin caps, sipping their own moonshine, stills in the basement. While in Paris, surfeited by pedestrians, blocked by literature, the writers evanesced.

The new State Capitol, which wasn't very far, resembled most eerily the U.S. Capitol in Washington, D.C. It was exactly three-fourths the size of the one in D.C. Karen complained that the roof of it got blown up every so often, because it looked so much like the one in the nation's capital. Movie companies used it to stage political thrillers. They blew up its roof every chance they got.

It occurred to me, looking at the replica, that Bill Clinton must have had plenty of practice in facing Congress by seeing this every day from the governor's office. We viewed it from the top of Capitol Street. An eleven-foot Henry Moore sculpture, called *Large Standing Figure Knife Edge*, stood just as its name implied, halfway between us and the building. It was like a weird gate, more funny than heroic, and quite incongruous. I'd expected nothing more daring than men on horses, the preferred statuary of the South. But there it was, Moore, the international avant-garde, pure cosmopolitanism. I have been startled more than once at modern public works rising from the most unexpected places. Small-town Americans, for all their vaunted conservatism, can have sudden joneses for the avant-garde, even if they complain for a while. Chicago is, of course, no small town, but the civic debate over its Picasso sculpture was typical. Eventually Chicagoans came to love it and now defend it most passionately.

Clinton's old house, now home of the new governor, was in Quapaw Quarter, an old neighborhood of stately trees, restored Victorians, and some ghost-ridden ruins. It stood a good distance behind two closed gates, but it looked friendly. Philip told me that the neighbors used to call the cops all the time when Bill's parties got too loud. "Uhm, Gov, you've got to turn down that music . . . the neighbors can't sleep."

Quapaw Quarter was at the moment the object of a restoration effort. At Fourteenth and Spring, a spruced-up mansion divided into apartments stood next to a church wall. It was Villa Marre, the house on the TV show *Designing Women*. It had been built by a saloon keeper in 1881, restored in 1964, and refurbished with Victorian furniture. As we went by, historic life-forms appeared: Southern belles in blue, pink, and white ruffled dresses were spilling noisily onto the porch, part of a wedding in period costume. Here was an interesting paradox: the streets were void of contemporaries but inhabited by people from the past. As cities go forth with Disney history for tourists, we may yet repopulate the streets with our ancestors. Faux ancestors, of course.

"I get the feeling," I said to the Martins, "that Little Rock has little nightlife, now that the Clintons have moved out."

My hosts were stung. Karen was emphatic: "You kidding? There is Juanita's Mexican Cantina, a pretty happening place. There is an okay local music scene at several bars. For a while, we didn't get much from the outside, mostly old war horses like the Marshall Tucker Band and .38 Special. We were ecstatic when Smashing Pumpkins came! But things are getting better."

"Yeah," added Philip, "at Juanita's tonight you can hear the Legendary Torpedoes and Techno-Squid."

"And there is Vino," said Karen, "the second best music place in town. They have their own microbrewery."

Philip and Karen lived in a pleasant, young professionals' neighborhood called Hillcrest. It was a hilly, residential area, with comfortable wooden homes. Philip pointed out the two neighborhood coffeehouses, The Morning Muffin and Caffe d'Roma, the first espresso place in Little Rock. It was next to the office of the vet who cared for Borck and Coal, their two dogs. From a hill near their house we could see the whole town. There were a good number of churches and hospitals. The Children's Hospital was a state-of-the-art institution, thanks to Hillary Clinton, who'd helped Little Rock to first-rate health care.

Hillcrest was homey and Little Rock did look like a good place to live. We walked past the Rep, a local repertory house that presented both standard fare and avant-garde theater. Just as Karen finished telling me about the brilliance of the Rep's director, Cliff Fannon Baker, we saw him on the porch of his house. He waved. Now that was a kind of persuasive coincidence. When synchronicity shows her hand, you are in tune with the universe.

We went past the Pyramid Gallery, a local artists' venue, the Calabash African Restaurant, and Sweden Cream, a fast-food place, home to Philip's favorite chili dog: Yankee Dog. We stopped at Wordsworth's bookstore, which had a healthy shelf of Arkansas authors proudly displayed. (It was true! Maybe people here still had time to tell stories, listen, and write. That kind of time is a commodity long gone in most places.)

Now what, with Swiss chefs, espresso joints, repertory theater, and African food, Little Rock didn't seem so square anymore. Still, hip 'n' happening is not what one would go to Little Rock for. Quite the contrary. You can find espresso and avant-garde anywhere, but the sense of down-home calm that was pervading this Saturday afternoon seemed to belong to another time, that time, long ago, when there was time. It was not a quality one can exactly bottle, measure, or sell, but that was precisely its value.

To make sure that they hadn't given me the wrong impression by exposing me to too much cultural diversity, the Martins took me to see the Christmas House, home to a Dr. Osborne, who festooned it every Christmas with 1.5 million *red* lights. Dr. Osborne's house, which caused traffic to back up for five miles, was a white-walled compound that looked like a tropical dictator's fort. The exaggerated height of the walls was made possible by building them on the one lawless day that had slipped between old and new zoning laws.

During winter, not far from the Christmas House, a drive-through living Nativity scene was on display, causing further traffic backups. Winter, it seemed, was Little Rock's more characteristic season: no espresso-avant-garde foolishness then.

But even this time of the year, I was privileged to observe hints of popular ease. On the side of the freeway, on the way to the airport, not far from Shorty Small's BBQ Ribs & Macho Nachos, there was a big tent with a sign proclaiming a sale on THE TREASURES OF THE ATOCHA. Mel Fisher's pirate-ship haul was on sale by the square centimeter. It made me smile. Henry Moore sculpture was fine, but this was more like the kind of stuff one expects from hometown America.

Philip said that a guy with a phoney French accent who called himself Jacques Le Mer had been advertising "the treasures" for a week.

"Can you believe it, a guy called Jacques the Sea?"

I could. And I was rather relieved, I must say. I was beginning to think that there was no respite from espresso. There is, but you have to hurry.

What Surrounds Little Rock: The Ozarks

Arkansas is the smallest state west of the Mississippi River, and one of the poorest in the country, but its Ozark Mountain culture in the north-central region is all its own. Eastern Arkansas, by contrast, is flat, bayou country reminiscent of Louisiana. The Ozarks are the mountains nearest to my adopted Louisiana home. I get, now and then, a sharp yen for rocks. And even for my grandmother, gone now for many years.

Going to the Ozarks is like going to visit your grandmother, provided that your grandmother, unlike mine, was an old-fashioned, pie-baking, herb-growing pioneer who used homemade brooms and poured ice cream from a dented churn. My grandmother was a severe Transylvanian who rarely spoke, but then she came from the jagged peaks of the Carpathians, not the gentle, old hills of the Ozarks. The kind of grandmother the Ozarks evoke may be a myth, but it is nonetheless soothing to imagine her, a balm to my nerve-racking electronic world. I was ready for the ministrations of an old, wise, and kind spirit.

The rolling hills that begin less than a hundred miles west of Little

Rock are indeed no forbidding Carpathian crags. They rarely rise above 2,500 feet, but they convey a down-home comfort, covered as they are with hardwoods and fields of sleepy wildflowers.

I inhaled deeply the scent of freshly mown hay as I drove up the gentle slopes. Even the cows that grazed dreamily through the ancient valleys seemed stitched on a sampler. And just to drive the point home, the '73 Oldsmobile in front of me was sporting the license plate GRANDMA. When I passed Grandma, who was doing about eighty, incidentally, I half-expected to be disappointed. But no, Grandma was indeed at the wheel. She was white-haired, with a face like an apple doll. She swung her head back and forth to some country tune on the radio, probably the same one I was listening to, given the fact that both stations receivable here on Route 65 to Mountainview were country. I passed Grandma just as Waylon Jennings told us that "in Texas Bob Wills is still the king," a sentiment I had no quarrel with. After all, I barely knew who either one of them was. Soon thereafter, I found myself behind a van whose wheel cover sported a bearded, dark-skinned Christ with the legend INDIAN AND PROUD OF IT. That too was fine by me. There were people other than grandmothers in Arkansas.

Driving the nearly empty winding road in the hot summer afternoon, I felt as if I had indeed left the din of contemporary America far behind. The only industry was the huge Maybelline factory, which flashed by on my left like eyeliner. After that, the only large-scale, mechanized endeavor was a cluster of long, low-squatting buildings full of millions of chickens waiting for Miss Goldie to turn them into frozen dinners. They didn't smell too good either, but the sky was blue and cloudless, and the flowers soon dispelled the disquieting scents.

Small-scale human industry was, however, present everywhere. Dotting both sides of the road were flea markets and gift shops. Everyone in Arkansas seemed to be selling his or her clothes. Between Little Rock and Mountain View, I counted a grand total of eighty-seven flea markets and yard sales. Folk of all ages, manning high-volume lemonade containers, stood behind piles of clothes and toys, fanning themselves with the *Arkansas Democrat-Gazette*.

The flea markets and yard sales were second in number only to gift shops. Between Little Rock and Mountain View I counted a grand total of one hundred and twenty gift shops, divided into folk art shops, rock shops, quilt shops, and what I have to call ultimate kitsch shops. The absolute ultimate U.K.S. was Beck's Gift Shop, located on Route 62 outside of Harrison. It flaunted the greatest display of lawn art ever assembled: spotted cement cows, black and white lawn jockeys, pairs of life-sized plaster swans, ceramic cacti with sombrero-clad Mexicans taking their siesta under them, an acre or so of cement chickens, plastic frogs, elephants, hobbits, and fountains. And that was just outside, in the yard. Inside, there were mazey rooms with overflowing shelves of trays of dusty rocks and minerals, dashboard art, marbles, magnets, and religious wood and stone carvings covering most of the major biblical instances. The proprietors, crowded behind a corner counter piled high with an overflow of chachkas, consisted of 1) a teenage daughter in short shorts whose face was invisible behind *The Star,* 2) a hunchbacked grandmother with her hair in rusted iron curlers standing behind an ancient cash register, 3) a gently ineffective giant of a man gluing price stickers on tiny dinosaurs, and 4) a cross-eyed, middle-aged woman whose sleepy look indicated kinship to the chair-bound nymphette. I bought two wooden eggs, a huge spotted marble, and a quartz rose, a transaction that lasted a satisfactorily long time because grandma pressed down most tentatively on the register keys and was flustered by the tax. No credit cards.

By contrast, the Ozark Folk Center at Mountain View concerned itself only with genuine folk crafts. The showpiece of the state's tourism industry, the center is a living museum of exhibits wherein genuine folk artists demonstrate the crafts of the region. There is also a 1,064-

seat musical auditorium where traditional folk musicals are staged. I drove up the curving driveway to the center in the late afternoon. The dappled light filtered through the trees, giving a shimmery, underwater look to the quiet surroundings.

A pleasant receptionist at the Ozark Folk Center Lodging office handed me a key to my cabin, a round wooden building ensconced in the woods. The clean, simple room was an overworked city drone's dream. Double-glass doors gave out onto a small grove of trees. The air-conditioning hummed sleepily. There was a Bible on the bedside table next to the lamp. The quiet of the twilight hour was broken only by the cry of a whippoorwill, a bird that likes to say its name over and over, like a political candidate. Perhaps that was how the state's greatest politician got started in Hope, Arkansas, a small town where, doubtlessly, the whippoorwill was king.

I followed a walking path through the woods to the music hall. The fireflies were out now, writing things on the purple air. Inside the hall, several hundred people, mostly over the age of seventy, were stomping their feet and whistling happily to the Apple Family's rendition of the "Orange Blossom Special," a perennial favorite, dating back to the time when the train had been a frightful miracle, a force of nature like a thunderstorm. Good roads did not come to Arkansas until the 1940s. The train must have been the only lifeline to the world for the mountain folks. The Apple Family, consisting of Brandon Apple, thirteen-year-old virtuoso; Brad Apple, paterfamilias; and John Beard and Shane Fudge, cousins, was filling the room with the sounds of guitar, violin, bass, and banjo. Square dancers, some from the audience, clambered onstage and proceeded to sway. The domed auditorium, festooned with cutouts of guitars, mandolins, banjos, and blue-jeaned silhouettes of country musicians, came to life.

The Apple Family was followed by balladeer Roger Birch, who sang sadly about sin and redemption, a simple tale that had the ancient couple in front of me clutch emotionally at each other. Hazel Thompson and Orville came up after that and sang, "Do You Ever Think of Me?," the Carter family song, which caused further sentiment. Bluestem, a passel of big-hatted cowboys from Kansas, sang cowboy favorites, including the wonderfully Hollywoodesque "Riding the Navajo Trail," which is as Western as the road runner cartoon. They also sang one of my faves, "They Call the Wind Maria," which is Greek tragedy chorus material. Next came Heritage, a three-piece white gospel band that sang three-part harmony about Jesus. The notion of white gospel had never crossed my mind before so I couldn't help noticing that compared to its black counterpart it was like dishwater to whiskey.

Speaking of which, it was just about then that I would have dearly liked to have a drink, but then I remembered. There wasn't any to be had. This was God-fearing country, and it was dry. The nearest liquor was fifty miles away. I banished the thought and studied the perfectly happy audience. There were mostly bald or shorthaired men in striped shirts or T-shirts standing by the side of their KMart-pattern-shirted and pastel-pantsed spouses. They looked contented, as if a lifelong practice of family values and the steady consumption of chicken-fried steak and mashed potatoes with white gravy were indeed the path to salvation.

In the evening, I experienced part of that practice at Lillian's Restaurant in Mountain View, where the chicken-fried steak and possum pie had been on special since 1959, the date of the founding. Lillian's had red-checkered plastic tablecloths and a profusion of old graters, wooden spoons, meat grinders, salt-and-pepper shakers, and milkers crowding shelves and the counter next to the register. Asked about the pie, the waitress laughed and said, "It doesn't have possum in it." It didn't. But the combination of the shortbread crust with layers of cream cheese, chocolate, and whipped cream wasn't exactly thrilling. It should have had possum in it. I have noticed that such wickedly oversweet desserts are found in abundance in strongly religious areas. In Utah, where Mormons don't drink coffee, there is a strong addiction to chocolate. Sugar is the vice of the righteous. And while I'm on the subject, I will now mention the food I had across the state of Arkansas, just to get it out of the way. Contrary to the claims of the tourist bureau, the "Ozark-cuisine" is neither delightful nor fresh. True, Granny's Restaurant in Mountain View closed at eight P.M., and Joshua's Ozark Restaurant was fast asleep by eight-thirty, so I may have missed something. But after Lillian's, the only bet was Eureka Pizza, open until nine P.M., a late hour that made the place a favorite with the teenage crowd. In the next three days I had perfunctory lunches at a series of undistinguished diner counters in small towns, though I could not be entirely objective because I'm a fish-eating vegetarian. I cannot testify to the pleasures of BBQ, which smelled enticing (even to me) and which was readily available. But after facing innumerable ketchup-splattered menus offering BBQ ribs, mashed potatoes and carrots, Ozark Bacon Burger, and Ham 'n' Cheese, I began to imagine that I might have to starve to death.

To be perfectly honest, I did eat at a very good restaurant in Eureka Springs, a Victorian town of Niagara Falls vintage some two hours from Mountain View. The place was called Cafe Armagost and, at very reasonable prices, it offered such fare as tofu picata, shrimp scampi, and filet mignon diablo with very fresh salad and fresh rolls of rye bread. My tofu was as soft as brains, and it came with capers and crisp asparagus with a tarragon-flavored hollandaise. Alas, between the pizza and this generic nouvelle cuisine spot, there was little else I found edible. There was no good reason for such failure. Fresh herbs grew in profusion, the streams were full of trout. But the only spice I noticed in the food was salt and the only fish, catfish! Even near the gorgeously beautiful Buffalo River wild area, there wasn't a trout to be had. For all that, an enormous amount of niceness and cheer came from the waitresses and cooks in these establishments, which almost made up for the gruel, but not quite.

Christina Wilcox was the gardener at the Ozark Cultural Center. Her beautiful flower and herb gardens swirled around the paths between the craftsmen's cabins. A breezy, shorthaired woman with a direct and refreshing manner, she took her visitors through bushes of orange, herb and chocolate mint, Russian sage, parsley, nasturtiums, geraniums, and a hundred other fragrant and useful plants. She told a group of kids from the Meadow Creek Project—a summer camp for ecologically minded would-be naturalists—not to "run in the grass or mash plants with your feet." Her love for the gardens was so obvious it gave her a luminous aura. The Meadow Creek Project kids hung around her like puppies. After getting a degree in horticulture and park management from Delgado College in New Orleans, she'd worked briefly for the New Orleans City Hall, but she soon tired "of watering the mayor's ficus," so she'd moved here to a (lower-paying) dream job.

Christina told me that the Meadow Creek Project was an idealistic community dedicated to sustainable energy, which ran its facilities on solar energy. The swarm of children roaming the fragrant little paradises between rocks put me in a wonderful mood. The old hills felt alive and hopeful.

Several log and stone cabins sat amid Christina's gardens. Craftsmen were at work inside them. Denny Maynard, the wood-carver, born in Boothills, Missouri, had been carving since the age of thirteen. He still had one of his first pieces, a carved wooden knife. For thirty years he'd been making roosters, mandolins, miniature wagons and horses, Indian flutes, pipes, and whatever struck his fancy. A gnomish, bearded fellow with round gold eyeglasses, he whittled as he talked to me. The cases on the walls of the cabin held his work as well as that of others, a gallery of ducks, gun stocks, family scenes carved out of whole tree roots, fanciful walking sticks. There were even wooden marbles, looking like stones.

Next door, Joe Jewell, luthier, was making a dulcimer, taking breaks only to play a tune on request on one of the many instruments he'd made. His dulcimers, mandolins, banjos, fiddles, guitars, and violins hung from the walls and sat on shelves, exuding a sweet aroma of fresh white oak, sassafras, ridgetop walnut, black cherry, sugar maple, and Ozark chinquapin, all local woods. He too was a forthcoming and delightful man who appeared to like children best of all. He asked two brothers, six and eight, if they wanted to hear a fast or a slow tune. "Fast," said the older one. "Slow," said the younger. "How about a medium slow fast?" suggested Joe, to everyone's satisfaction.

At the broom shop, a lean, muscular, bearded John Perry was squeezing stiff sheaves of straw tightly and winding seventeen-inch galvanized wire around them. He made oak brooms with red and white handles. The morning crowd gathered about the broom maker seemed oddly quiet, as if witnessing some forbidden ritual, not the rather domestic and intimate manufacture of the world's most common object. Common yes, but also magical. I remembered the reassuring swish of my grandmother's broom over the flagstone floor of her house in Alba Iulia, Romania. And the broom of our Hungarian maid on Elizabethstrasse in Sibiu. You cannot underestimate the broom as a source of memory for those of us still lucky enough to have been born in the pre-vacuum-cleaner days. In Paris, street sweepers still employ the old straw brooms on the streets, but the straw is plastic.

The crafts of the Ozarks weren't just a carefully preserved historical activity. They were everywhere. On West Main Street in Mountain View (next door to Lillian's) was the Ozark Rocker & Wood Company, a splendid storeroom of homemade rockers, chairs, and benches at very reasonable prices.

On a weekday, I might have driven through Leslie, Arkansas, without taking much notice of anything, except perhaps the cheap ($1.07 per gallon) gas at the two pumps manned by a friendly man who waved away the two extra cents I didn't have in change. But today, on a Saturday, Leslie was celebrating Homecoming.

In a grassy field off the main street, young men with baseball caps were throwing horseshoes. Tables and booths packed with crafted objects crowded the center of town from the street to the bandstand. I was attracted by a display of small sculptures. A serious-looking sixteen-year-old boy named Sam Price told me that he and his mom, Patty Price, made them. One was a house carved from a hollow tree ring with moss, nuts, and a butterfly perched on the rim of a wood mushroom. Sam said that they also used stuffed birds, broken eggs, and feathers. Each of the Prices' sculptures had a handwritten poetic explanation by Patty, describing the materials and the significance of the work. The intricate, hobbit-like, magic objects sold for seventeen to thirty-five dollars and had been made specially for the Leslie Homecoming. Other tables displayed potpourri bags for two dollars, handcrafted clocks, dolls, quilts, cut-out painted wooden cows, pillows, and a variety of domestic implements.

In the middle of the street (closed to cars), a troupe of square dancers moved to the bluegrass strains of a boom box sitting on the back of a pickup truck. Old men with straw boaters sat in folding chairs in front of the shuttered storefronts, watching the middle-aged cloggers in their lace-trimmed dresses with red fringed blouses and headbands. When the Spare Change Band took the stage, everyone crowded up in front to dance. Some people had shaving foam or whipped cream in their hair and in their clothes from a pie fight I hadn't seen. But when I returned to my car, there was shaving foam or whipped cream on the windshield. The band leader asked everyone in front of the stage to line up in two facing rows. Two eight-men lines formed, each member armed with an egg. To the strains of "Achy Breaky Heart," the egg toss began. The bursting eggs soon eliminated all but four of the best, who had to step back farther each time they caught an egg unbroken. Eventually, the four contestants left were so far from one another they spanned the whole field. "Them Richardson boys are brothers," said the band leader into the microphone. "They been tossin' green persimmons since they were babies." But the Richardson brothers were eliminated, leaving two major leaguers who pitched ten eggs at each other from about a mile away before one of them, Jedediah Kirsh, won the contest.

Driving out of Leslie, the road rose and fell through the gentle Ozarks, past sweet hilltop cemeteries swathed in wildflowers, Queen Anne's lace, day lilies, black-eyed Susans, wild roses, columbines, mimosas, wild grapes. A hawk was floating over the treetops. I wanted to pull over and go to sleep. Mountain meadows always make me want to lie down in the deep grass, to sleep and to dream. But I kept going. Now and then, gravel roads led to quilters' cottages or white Baptist churches. I drove past fallen barns, cows eating sweet clover, horses swinging their tails lazily to chase away flies. A lone weeping willow stood in front of a wooden house on a gentle slope. A sign said, SHII-TAKE MUSHROOMS, 2 MILES. It was incongruous. What was this yuppie mushroom of Japanese origin doing here amid Ozark brooms and flea markets? But there wasn't much that was incongruous. The rare satel-lite-dish antenna. Mostly I reveled in the view of green valleys and mountains from above, views that were good to my city-weary soul. The strains of "Old Time Gathering," which I'd bought at the Ozark

Folk Center, filled the air with the sweet sounds of the hammer dulcimer, Autoharp, guitar, mandolin, fiddle, and banjo. For a piney
stretch, at a higher altitude, there was a smoky smell of burning wood
and cooking.

Eureka Springs, Arkansas, is a Victorian resort town that has been
catering to tourists since the waning days of the last century. It was a
jumble of toy cottages, mighty mansions, steep walking paths, rock
shrines carved around springs and, of course, gift shops, music halls,
and quaint little museums. I put up at the Inn of the Ozarks, a Best
Western motel with startling views of the mountains.

Flower-bedecked guest houses featuring hot tubs, Victorian salons,
chandeliers, and lace curtains crowded the narrow streets. Judging by
the posters glued to the lampposts, the cultural life of the town revolved
around a number of music festivals and fairs. The most popular of these
was the Great Passion Play, an open-air reenactment of Christ's mis-
fortune. The performance took place at the foot of the immense statue
of the Christ of the Ozarks, which was visible from every place in
Eureka Springs. The giant squat sculpture had been made in the like-
ness of a certain Mr. Smith, who'd paid for it, and had originally been
so tall that airplanes were in danger. Consequently, it'd had its legs
shortened, so that the Christ of the Ozarks, illuminated at night, looked
squat and somewhat Polynesian. I don't know whether the passion play
itself matched its Bavarian counterpart in anti-Semitism, but it is ru-
mored that (some years) it did. Another major Baptist entertainment
takes place at the (foreshortened) feet of the Ozarks' Christ, namely
the *Anita Bryant Show*, a religious musical revue headlined by the right-
wing Queen of Orange Juice herself. The area abounds in Baptist Boys'
Camps, Christian Scout Centers, and other wholesome groupings, so
that the entertainments are never without an audience.

At night, the Victorian cottages seemed embroidered rather than built: they were embraced by a profusion of cultivated blooms in the shapes of hearts and other topiary sentiments. Their stained-glass windows, lace curtains, and teardrop crystal chandeliers bespoke the sentimental Victorian style that had reached its apogee (and its end) in the drawings of Aubrey Beardsley.

At the end of the Eureka historical district, I came upon a beautiful Catholic church called St. Elizabeth's. It was magically bathed in moonlight. The life-size statue of a beautiful woman called *St. Elizabeth of Hungary* stood at the top of the path leading down to the church. Statues representing the stations of the cross lined the path—exceptionally well-rendered full marble figures. I attended the service in progress, but I was disappointed when the deacon delivered a sermon that sounded more fire-and-brimstone Baptist than Catholic. He complained that after thirty years of giving his children, grandchildren, and great-grandchildren birthday presents related to Jesus, he was beginning to run out of ideas. No wonder. The idea that one can render onto children an endless stream of Christian kitsch was an insult to the cultural richness of the Mother Church.

The only place offering even remotely wicked possibilities was the Magnolia Bar & Grill at the New Orleans Hotel (naturally!). Deeply alienated souls were crowded onto the plastic banquettes of this establishment, drinking grudgingly doled out portions of whiskey and recalling small-town injustices and the vexing oblivion of tourists. I also paused briefly at the Sweet Spring, so named because courting couples used to come here in the Gay Nineties. (The other Gay Nineties!). I watched from the door of a photo shop as an elderly couple squeezed into Belle Epoque skirts and trousers to pose for an old-time photograph that made them look like their grandparents. In fact, the whole town seemed consumed by this desire for retrogeniture.

Next morning, another fine summer day, though hotter than the previous days ("hay-haulin' weather," I overheard someone say), I headed out to the Buffalo River National Park area. Route 21 to Ponca on the Buffalo River area was pretty wild. There were few signs of human habitation. In the early evening, I reached the Buffalo Outdoor Center, a friendly place run by folks who lived next door in a trailer. I was handed the key to the Buffalo Outdoor Center's lodging and given complicated directions to the place. Rock faces rose on the sides of the small road as I searched for my cabin. After losing my way several times, I made it to the Presidential Cabin, a wood-hewn, brand-new dwelling on a mountainside. The interior was well appointed with a stone fireplace, Arkansas Queen Anne furniture that smelled of freshly hewn wood, a loft reached by a spiral staircase, and a large whirlpool bath. The view out the window was of a stupendous succession of mountain ridges whose shadows played on each other's sides. In these wild surroundings, the amenities were comforting: there was a TV, a VCR, family-entertainment tapes, good loudspeakers. The walls of the Presidential Cabin were covered with presidential plates sporting Ike and Mamie, John and Robert Kennedy, and Lyndon Johnson. Above the fireplace was a framed portrait of the first Arkansan and his wife, Hillary, as well as two letters to the founders of the Buffalo Outdoor Center, Mike and Evelyn Mills, from former governor and then President Clinton, thanking them for the invitation to spend the night and wishing them good luck.

I watched the magnificent sunset from the porch, uncorked the champagne bottle thoughtfully left by my hosts, and listened to the silence broken only now and then by a bird. Around midnight, I drove down in the moonlight to the Buffalo River. The river snaked between huge dark boulders. I heard campers laughing. I crept stealthily past them until I found a pool formed by a small waterfall that came crashing down between two rocks. I left my clothes on the bank and dove in. There is nothing to compare to the feeling of floating in a mountain pool under the stars.

Next morning, I hiked a couple of miles through the forest. Long strips of fog were lying between the blue-gray mountains waiting for the sun. I jumped from rock to rock along a creek and sat in a cave looking out on the dappled forest floor. I saw a fox and a bear cub.

San Antonio: The South's Border Culture

If Little Rock, Arkansas, and what surrounds it are the white Baptist quintessence of the South, San Antonio, at the other extreme, is another South entirely, the Latin South. Its mythology is layered and still being formed: in microcosm it mirrors America. The legends of our founding are often confused with the Hollywood products of the same name, and the goodwill to incorporate newer myths is sometimes painful, but quite often comic.

The first time I went to San Antonio, I had a fight with my ex-wife at the Alamo. I don't remember what the tiff was about, but I was no more willing to surrender than the brave Texan defenders of the fort who fought the Mexican troops of General Santa Ana to the bitter end. When it looked like neither side was going to relent, my son Lucian, who was then six years old, shouted: "Forget the Alamo!" That immortal shout, the very opposite of the one that has come down to us in history, did put a cessation to the hostilities. Consequently, I never forgot the Alamo.

The fort spans 250 years of turbulent history involving the Spanish who founded it, the Texans who defended it, the Mexicans who attacked it, and the Native Americans who felt quite ambiguous about everybody else's claims. The Alamo is the most famous tourist attraction in Texas for reasons that go beyond its modest physical size. There is something palpably strange here, ghostly even. This strangeness has not gone unnoticed. A book entitled *The Haunted Alamo*, by Robert and Anne Powell Wlodarski, claims that the ghosts of Davy Crockett and other defenders of the siege haunt the dingy environs. There are inexplicable sightings and mysterious bloodstains. Portraits are often askew and historical artifacts move from their places. If this is the case, our little domestic fight may have been caused by these restless spirits. Maybe we were possessed.

I do remember things other than the Alamo. I remember the sparkling river walk in the downtown area where we sat listening to a mariachi band and eating tamales at an outdoor restaurant. I remember a tourist boat along the river, guided by a beautiful Mexican girl with black hair, who told an eerie story in a voice barely above a whisper. The tourists sat quietly, enthralled by her tale and by a gorgeous sunset. By the time we left San Antonio, we were at peace. Something mild and wise in the air had made us forget our differences.

San Antonio is a city with a long history of reconciling different people and their proudly distinct cultures. Native Americans, Mexicans, and Americans have forged something new here. The name of this new cultural, geographical, and political phenomenon is Border Culture. Border Culture is something still being born; it exists now in an expectant readiness, defined by poetry, fiction, art, handicraft, and new or rediscovered uses of space. Border culture is urban to the core, with all the hard-edged beat and pavement-hard strife of the city, but its sentimental heart longs for the Sonora Desert and the Andes Mountains.

San Antonio's Guadalupe Art Center's Inter-American Book Fair and Literary Festival is a yearly event that brings a stellar gathering of writers into town for a three-day program of readings and discussions.

In 1996, among the participants were some of the best representatives of emerging Border Culture, such as Ana Castillo, Rudolfo Anaya, Luis Rodriguez, Joseph Bruchac, Naomi Shihab Nye, Alberto Rios, and Deborah Paredez. They were poets, novelists, and storytellers. Their work was rich with the idioms of Spanish and English, a magical fusion of sounds that sounded at times like a whole new language. They were bringing to English the soulfulness of Spanish and importing into Spanish the precision of English. In these days of acrimonious political debate about the character of our nation, they embodied and exemplified

DAVID GRAHAM: *99 Bottles on the Wall*
(COURTESY OF THE PHOTOGRAPHER)

the beauty and power of culture-meshing, and they did this in poetry and song, not cliches and ideology. Here, for instance, is part of a poem by Deborah Paredez, giving voice to the Border's struggle for identity:

> *Yeah, you and me, sister, we know about boundaries,*
> *we live on them, in them, in the mountains between*
> *two cultures converging like massive plates of earth colliding,*
> *neither willing to subduct, to submit. Here at this range*
> *of cooled magma, we reside, bound to the rocks by hyphen-*
> *ated American identities.*

I have a hyphenated identity myself, though it rarely occurs to me to call myself a Romanian-American writer. I just say "writer" and let the hyphen hang out there for anyone interested. The institutionalized deadness of the word *multiculturalism* is partly responsible for the flood of adversary rhetoric of our identity politics. Ideologues are quite at home in "isms." Poetry, on the other hand, baffles and disorients the xenophobes. In preparation for meeting my hyphenated colleagues— mostly Mexican-American, but also one Arab-Mexican, and one Anglo-American—I'd bought a book called *The Late Great Mexican Border* to read on the airplane. It is a collection of essays and stories about the Mexican-U.S. border. I was moved to tears by a story about children living at the Tijuana garbage dump. It was called "None of Them Talk About Their Dreams," by Max Aguilera-Hellweg. In this story, the Mexican side of the border is light-years away from the American side, divided by bleak poverty. These children's world was hope-less, far from the shiny promises of NAFTA, far from the might of business that was booming on both sides of the border.

Luckily, I read the next story, called "The Last of the Border Lords," by Dick J. Reavis, the saga of the rise and fall of Octaviano

"Chito" Longoria, one of the border's greatest business geniuses. This story was the very opposite of the other; it made everything seem possible and miraculous. The Longoria business empire rose for over a century from the peculiar conditions of the border to benefit two countries.

Between these two stories there was a vast world of complexity and differences, almost as vast as the 2,000-mile Mexican-U.S. border. The border was a place of danger, opportunity, and adventure. It had its own customs, it was evolving its own language and, in all likelihood, it had its own laws and cuisine.

I was famished when I got off the plane, so I was more than grateful when one of the fellows who met me, Edward Leal, asked: "Do you like Mexican food?"

I looked at him quite astonished. "Of course. What else can you eat in San Antonio? That's like going to France and being asked, 'Do you like French food?'" The French would never think to ask it, because they assume that their cuisine is glorious. (And I'm glad that they don't ask, because I *don't* like French food. Last time I was in Paris, I found satisfaction only after discovering a Tex-Mex restaurant on rue St. Dennis. Let the French glory in their over-buttered, rolled, punched, sauced, drowned, beaten, and tortured ex-vegetables and former meats: something American in me calls for the hearty fare of my continent!)

I knew right away that Edward and I would hit it off. This was made plainly evident when we sat at one of Rosario's Mexican Cafe y Cantina's patio tables. It was the Day of the Dead, *Día de los Muertos*, which is a huge religious festival of remembrance among Mexicans. Rosario's Cantina was displaying an altar for the dead and an extraordinary profusion of flowers and angels created by the artist Sylvia Saldana-Sanchez. Garlands of dried chiles festooned the walls. Gleaming copper pots hung between them. Selena, the murdered border goddess of Tex-Mex music, was on the radio. I remembered seeing her flower-bedecked portrait at Los Angeles's South Central Market, surrounded by weeping teenage girls. She now had a full-fledged cult on both sides of the border.

"The whole neighborhood has altars for the dead. There will be a candlelit procession tonight on South Alamo Street," Edward told me. "You can remember your own dead, if you wish, with a candle or an offering."

The timing was right. Barely two days before, I'd gone to the funeral of my friend, the poet Jim Gustafson, in Detroit. Jim had been one of my best city-tramping pals in San Francisco, when we were both young and full of surging poetry. We would go up and down the hills of that burg, endlessly undoing and remaking the world in words. We knew every café, every bar, every youthful haunt, every odd place from which to watch and consider. We admired girls, women, architecture, the Zen Garden and Garden for the Blind in Golden Gate Park. Jim, a city boy par excellence, had moved back to Detroit where he'd been born, and life in that Midwestern toughness had been too much for him.

I would make an offering for Jim that would join all the others and sail along with everyone's prayers. I had always thought, foolishly it turned out, that the *Día de los Muertos* festival was like Halloween. It's not. It is a major religious event with ritual art made specifically for the occasion. People remember their dead with flowers, candies, and breads. Edward told me that the "day" was actually three days: November first, second, and third.

"They say that November first is for remembering grown-ups, November second is for children, and November third is for those . . . who were killed by witchcraft." He looked me over to make sure that I could take this news.

I could. My poet friend Jim Gustafson had been killed by witchcraft: poverty. Poverty is witchcraft deployed against the poor and ten-derhearted. Jim was a poor poet and the world doesn't like poets. It kills them with witchcraft. But I didn't tell Edward any of this. Instead, I said, much as I had when he'd asked me if I liked Mexican food: "We're on the border, aren't we? It's the border between fact and imag-ination."

Edward was supposed to interview me for Texas Public Radio, KPAC 88.3 FM, San Antonio's Public Radio Station, but, he told me, sighing, "The station has just been hit by lightning."

"Hey, don't worry about it. Happens everywhere I go."

"It happens a lot," he went on, "Texas storms. They call this kind of lightning 'border snakes.' "

I fell like a ravenous border snake about the huge plate of chile rellenos in front of me. The huge chiles had cheese and raisins in them and had been lightly fried in a crisp corn butter. Radio could wait. I'd never heard of raisins in relleno before.

"A central Mexican dish," commented Edward who, for the next three days, turned out to be a fountain of esoteric information.

The Guadalupe Arts Center Annual Bookfair and Literary Festival Book Fair was unfolding in a cavernous hall of the San Antonio Con-vention Center. Every city has one of these now; while their multi-purpose usefulness is a boon to city coffers, I can't help feeling that I'm in a huge tomb every time I'm inside one of these buildings. They are like Egyptian pyramids or spaceships. Large enclosed public spaces, whether domed stadiums or convention centers, are frightening to me precisely for their capacity to hold immense crowds. It would be so easy to shut the doors and kill everyone inside, like despots once did in the Balkans. Or, conversely, lift everyone into space or into heaven when the lift-off order or the Rapture comes.

Publishers of regional literature, small press magazines, and bilingual books were displaying their wares, wholly unaware of what haunted me. Or maybe not. Author readings went on in a partitioned area of the big hall.

George Farias, the owner of the Borderlands Bookstore, gave me a copy of what he said was the oldest book ever written about San Antonio. It was a swashbuckling history entitled *City of Flaming Adventure: The Chronicle of San Antonio*. I tried to pay him for it, but he'd take no money. I love old booksellers. I have known dozens and most of them are crazy. Some of them refuse to sell you books if they think you aren't worthy of them. Others refuse to take money. I shook George's hand and moved on.

My old friend Bobby Byrd, the publisher of Cinco Punto Press, greeted me effusively and handed me a copy of *The Late Great Mexican Border*, before I had a chance to tell him that I'd just been reading it on the airplane. Bobby's press, based in El Paso, puts out an astonishing number of border-related publications. The latest was *Women and Other Aliens: Essays from the U.S.-Mexican Border*. Like most literary enterprises, Bobby's runs on a lot of heart and very little money. Book publishing in the United States today is dominated by major corporate houses and distribution systems that make little room for the kind of fresh work that Cinco Punto brings to light. Such books are usually available only to dedicated lovers of literature, but unlike many of the perishable items in the airport paperback racks, they last a lot longer, and have a better chance of being read many years from now.

"Have you had lunch?" Bobby asked me.

Well, I had just eaten at Rosario's but I thought I'd have a cup of coffee. Bobby left his display in the hands of his daughter and of her little baby, and we crossed Alamo Street to the Riverwalk Center. Bobby took me to a *German* deli! That was a surprise but, by now, I had given up on any preconceived ideas about San Antonio.

When we returned to the festival, the book fair was in full swing. The organizer of the Guadalupe festival, Bryce Milligan, was a bearded, serious-looking man who went about his many tasks as if the world depended on his next move. When I encountered him, Bryce was in the middle of directing a complicated scenario involving booksellers, readers, and airplane schedules. Bryce surveyed all this activity with intense concentration, but dropped everything when I asked him about the writing history of San Antonio. This turned out to be one of his passions.

"San Antonio has a writing history going back to the nineteenth century. We were renowned for our mild winters, so writers came, among throngs of other Northerners, looking for the beneficent climate to cure them. Sidney Lanier, the Georgia poet who was suffering from consumption, came in 1872. O'Henry founded a newspaper here in 1894. He wasn't sick, he just found the place congenial. Other people came to escape oppression. During the Mexican Revolution, Mexican writers in exile found here the freedom to write. I'll take you to the Liberty Bar later. Robert Frost, John Dos Passos, and Daniel Shorr all drank there. . . ."

That afternoon we adjourned to the Liberty Bar, where I had a great gruyere and tomato sandwich on thick rye bread with a side of pico de gallo to go with my Guinness. Bryce gave me a paper he'd written called "A Century of Writing in San Antonio." It begins: "It has often been said that San Antonio is an excellent place to write but a rotten place to be a writer."

He explained this apparent contradiction by claiming that writers were attracted to San Antonio's natural beauty, but found it difficult to survive economically. This was no less true today, despite the great many literary presses and events such as this festival.

"Sure, Bryce," I said, "but the difficulty of surviving as a writer is not specific to San Antonio. You can say the same about just any place.

Nobody's parents tell their kids to become writers. Everybody knows that glorified poverty attends our glorious profession."

Poverty was the last thing you'd think about if you were a guest of the Columns on Alamo Bed & Breakfast, where the festival quartered me. This charming colonnaded manse in the historic King William neighborhood was the kind of place I sometimes fantasize about living in when I run away from my responsibilities and worries. My sumptuous Victorian room gave out onto a balcony looking out into a shaded street of old homes. The genteel proprietors, Ellenor and Art Link, welcomed me with genuine warmth. "It's all writers in here now," exclaimed Art, as if this were the most wonderful thing in the world.

Next morning, over breakfast, when a few of us sipped tentatively at our orange juices and coffees, Ellenor intervened gracefully in our grumpy discussion, as if writers were just regular folk. Well, in a sense we are, but not in the morning. Being born again each day in a difficult world is one of the hardest moments in a writer's life. Especially if the writer was up late, sampling the brews at the Liberty Bar in the enlightened company of Edward Leal and Bobby Byrd. Be that as it may, Ellenor's kindness and her incredible huevos rancheros contributed positively to my matinal reentry.

The King William neighborhood, settled originally by Germans, was full of splendid houses. I had the pleasure of strolling along the river with poet Joseph Bruchac, a Native American poet and storyteller, who is fond of the local architecture. He pointed out the Anton Wulff house, an imposing structure, with a square tower, featuring a cast-iron rose arbor. Originally the residence of a lumber baron, it was now the headquarters of the San Antonio Conservation Society. Next to it was the Blondin House, a neoclassical building with tall Ionic columns. In the bright, blue morning, with a cup of coffee in my hand,

I felt keenly the beauty of San Antonio. Bruchac, who had walked along the river many times, told me that he had identified twelve species of butterflies on his walks.

The city of San Antonio understood early what many American cities are just beginning to think about: value the river. Cities have always grown alongside the shores of a river or another body of water that served their commercial and civic needs. Wise old cities like Paris have always known that the river is more than a thoroughfare for the passage of goods. A city's river is also a spiritual artery, a place for citizens to stroll and think, reflect, remember, and exercise. The river focuses the soul of a city.

As we came closer to downtown, music began to drift in from sidewalk cafés. A Peruvian band was rending the morning air with crisp mountain melodies. The sound of flutes mingled with the wavelets of water stirred by a light breeze. Farther down, a German choir from Milwaukee was putting its heart into a religious hymn in German. Not far from the choir, a lone longhaired guitarist strummed and sang a folk song to a closely knit group of tourists. A slow-moving boat appeared, piloted by the beautiful Mexican girl of long ago. Well, maybe. Memory is a funny thing. But she *was* beautiful.

Downtown, it became obvious that San Antonio was a prosperous American city. Still, I was surprised to hear that it was among the top twenty largest cities in the United States. There was a small-town feeling here, despite the snazzy office buildings and the shiny new Alamodome, which sat like a glittering fly trap, waiting to catch a stray NFL team. But I was not surprised to hear that San Antonio Spurs players were so nice that the flamboyant, many-hued Dennis Rodman had to leave for someplace tougher. San Antonio *is* nice. Perhaps the city fathers ought to consider making a permanent home for the Guadalupe Arts Center in the Alamodome. Writers, it seems to me, are some of the toughest people in the world. When despots kill us, our writings demolish them. And if we go into space, well, maybe we'll have a whole new audience.

I imagine that aliens might reconstruct the story of all that was interesting on our home planet by hearing Ana Castillo read. She read stories that had the lyrical density of poetry and the tough wisdom of survival. Their wistful melancholy brought forcefully to the fore the dilemma and power of having roots in two worlds, the Anglo and the Latino in her case, the American and Romanian in mine. Meditating on this condition is one of the most urgent tasks in our emerging borderless world.

Outside, after her performance, the *Día de los Muertos* procession was setting out for its pilgrimage along South Alamo Street. Feeling like I was still inside one of Ana Castillo's stories, I joined the marchers behind the bright candlelit altar being carried by masked celebrants. We stopped by the San Angel Folk Art Gallery where a traditional *Día de los Muertos* altar invited everyone to bring photos of their dear departed ones, bread, and flowers. I laid a daisy there for Jim. The Studio Gallo, a bit farther down, had a Day of the Dead show, featuring altars, paintings, photos, sugar skulls, and flowers. At every place the procession stopped there was food and drink for the marchers, and musicians played traditional Mexican folk songs. The night throbbed with music and an insistent sweetness. The flickering candlelight made America and its car-filled highways seem very far away all of a sudden. It was an illusion, of course. But this was the border, the casa of illusions.

Some of us capped the evening at the Blue Star Brewing Company. A long table full of poets and artists can be an awesome thing. A sheet of paper began circulating and everyone wrote something and then passed it to the next person. This type of poetic collaboration, practiced in taverns worldwide since writing began, is called "an exquisite corpse." Bryce Milligan, Edward Leal, Santiago Garcia, Deborah Paredez, Sarah Cordova . . . are just a few of the signatures I am able to make out at the bottom of the sheet. The collaboration itself pulsed with the magic of the moment. Here are a few lines:

> *laughter rings to the bottom*
> *that's how I lived that winter*
> *the danger excites me*
> *we live inside carousels*

No one knew who wrote what line and no one could say precisely what this poem was about. But there it was, flickering like candlelight in the fantasy land of the border.

On the third day, Edward Leal got me up early. We had breakfast at a little cantina in a Hispanic neighborhood of San Antonio. We were hoping to watch people visit the graves of their relatives at the San Fernando Cemetery nearby. The Guadalupe Church on El Paso Street was full of people dressed in holiday clothes. I bought a decorated funeral bread from a little boy. He told me that his mom and aunt had been baking all night. The bread was fresh and smelled wonderful.

Suddenly, Edward changed his mind. He announced that we were not going to the San Fernando Cemetery after all. We were going to visit his grandmother's grave in the country. It was a blue, mild San Antonio morning, and the prospect of a drive into the country delighted me. We left San Antonio and after a stretch of freeway driving we turned onto a red dirt road and began following a creek. Along the way, Edward told me his family history. His grandparents had owned vast tracts of land in this area, and the place was still dotted with his numerous relatives. Edward himself had twelve siblings. We passed a ghost town by the railroad tracks. A closed bank and feed store were overgrown with weeds. Edward's nostalgia for his country childhood was exotic to me. I'm an only child from the city.

At last we came to the Leal family cemetery at the end of Leal Road. *Leal* is a Spanish name, pronounced Leh-ahl. The cemetery was already festooned with flowers and the graves had been cleaned. A couple of Edward's relatives were raking the dirt around some of their kin. We found his grandmother's grave and Edward put the fresh bread on it. "It's from Andrei," he said.

"Thank you," I said, when we were driving back.

"No, thank *you*," he said.

I had no idea what he was thanking me for, but that's the border for you. You don't have to understand everything.

The Festival closed on Sunday night with another reading and more camaraderie. On the way back, I leafed through some of the books I had collected, and came upon this poem by Bobby Byrd, in a collection titled *On the Transmigration of Souls in El Paso*.

> *Maybe we will be elsewhere*
> *maybe not, but*
> *we will be somewhere*
> *where*
> *the birds, like the sun and the moon,*
> *go about their business,*
> *and we go about ours*

It seemed a fitting farewell. The best places always make you feel like all is well with the world.

PART THREE

WALKER EVANS: *Royal Baking Powder Steps*
(J. PAUL GETTY MUSEUM, LOS ANGELES)

The Language of American Cities

Cities speak many languages. To the traveler and the tourist, they speak a shorthand intended to relieve them of their money. In exchange they experience the frisson of the "exotic." They carry back a modicum of sentiment and a bag full of souvenirs and photographs. It is a gentle operation that leads, in the best of cases, to a slight loss of provincialism and a lessening of xenophobia. The outer layer of this benefit is wrapped in the tourist's own smug self-satisfaction. This is what Milan Kundera, the Czech novelist, calls kitsch. Kitsch is harmless in the late days of our millennium: self-satisfaction is short-lived now, thanks to the never-ending streams of anxiety produced by ever-newer forms of the exotic. The tourist with last year's slides is instantly eclipsed by the newer slides of his neighbor.

To architects, cities speak in the language of space and history. To sociologists, cities are "people-books," legible by numbers. To adventurers, they hold the promise of anonymous encounters and are a dense forest of furtive gazes. Every city has an erotic "book of looks," that ranges from the skimpy pamphlet of someplace like Iowa City to the multi-volume opus of Paris. To lovers of poetry they are maps of the lives of the poets who lived there. To businessmen and thieves, they are alphabets of locked wealth that might be sprung open by their ingenuity. To the wealthy leisure class, they speak the language of real estate opportunities, the charm of the pied-à-terre. I have a friend who has pied-à-terres in New York, Paris, Prague, and Boulder: he has as many feet on earth as a centipede.

In addition to these languages, cities also deploy language itself in myriad forms: advertising, graffiti, historical plaques, epitaphs on tombstones, street names, movie and theater posters, restaurant names. The visual presence of this constant language fascinated Walker Evans, one of America's greatest photographers. His work is indispensable to understanding the American city in the twentieth century.

Reading Walker Evans's America

Modernism was in awe of the Word, an awe matched only by its total mistrust of what words had come to mean in the bourgeois world: debased in advertisements, spoken without meaning on the streets, issuing fully stillborn from the mouths of politicians, sprayed like cream swirls on the rococo pastries of art. The twentieth century busted out in a babble of words whose din was overcome briefly only by the loud explosions of World War I, the trench war, the war of dynamite Mr. Nobel. Perched there on the rim of the black crater left by bombs, the Dada poets and writers crowed their ironic songs. The Dadaists were refugees from the great metropolises of the West, which had been sucked up in the vortex of war. Crowded in Zurich, Switzerland, at the periphery of European culture, they composed the swan song of Western civilization, inventing the future in the process. The Dada poem was made out of cut-up newspapers. The Dada picture was made out of cut-up advertisements. And collage became the preeminent response to the faux seriousness of commerce and its forced jollity on the cusp of disaster. And it was up to photography to rescue whatever lyric lament was still there. Brassaï and Atget's Paris unfolds nostalgically, ironically, rain drenched, absurd, and touching, signaling both the end and the beginning of a Great Something.

After the Great War, a black-and-white giddiness seized the world. With the crater at its back, Walker Evans's generation was launched on a high-minded quest that was simultaneously frivolous and cabalistic. James Joyce was the priest of the new religion of art, which raised the vulgate to a dizzying perfection. Walker Evans was raised on the High Modernists and his beginnings were steeped in literature. Born in 1903, he caught the full force of the Gilded Age in Paris in 1926–1927. He intended to be a writer and his friendships were literary. He attended lectures at the Sorbonne and was no doubt conversant with the Dada and Surrealist revolutions. He worked briefly at Nadar's studio in Paris and took snapshots with a Kodak vest-pocket camera. This apprenticeship is significant in view of the common perception of Walker Evans as, chiefly, the documentarian of Depression-era America. He was that, but the stubborn pull of esthetic modernism is ever-present in all his work. Active in the air of postwar Europe were the two faces of modernism: the highly colored, poetic, gravity-defying, and very French manipulation of reality in order to achieve a sur-reality, and the dead earnest, plebe-loving, messianic fervor of Ezra Pound and various weighty fascist-communist futurisms. On this side of things one must count also the constructivist revolution with its technological fetishes. While surrealism floundered in the thirties, the ominous seriousness of the second strain prevailed. And the world, never very friendly to fiction, took itself very seriously indeed.

Back in New York in 1927, Evans lived in Brooklyn Heights and met Hart Crane. There is this in *The Bridge*, Crane's famous work inspired by the Brooklyn Bridge:

> *I think of cinemas, panoramic sleights*
> *With multitudes bent toward some flashing scene*

Never disclosed, but hastened to again,
Foretold to other eyes on the same screen;

and Thee, across the harbor, silver-paced
As though the sun took step of thee, yet left
Some motion ever unspent in thy stride,
Implicitly thy freedom staying thee!

Crane opposes the transience of the moving picture to the permanence-in-flight of the bridge, hoping to found a new classical ethic on these modern phenomena. The ethical concern is thoroughly American and this is where American modernism parts with its European kin. America, which was way ahead of Europe in the certainty of its allegiance to the new, was morally conservative. The architecture of the Brooklyn Bridge, like that of New York City or that of Chicago, for that matter, put into action the principles of modern art without an attendant hope for social or political revolution. Or, at least, not of the kind predicted by the purists. What Hart Crane wrote, despite the complexities of his philosophical qualms, was an ode to the bridge, a Whitmanesque ode to the marvelous engineering of that soaring shape. The functioning tensions were those of speed, between the relative stillness of architecture and the seeming unfolding of the moving picture. *The Bridge* was published with three photographs by Walker Evans, photographs that make unapologetic use of the many formal delights of the span in different lights. They are pictures of the bridge in motion, a moving picture of architecture. Evans's photography situated itself between architecture and the motion picture. These two poles, architecture and unfolding story, remained constant for him throughout the five decades of his career.

The twentieth century is the American century: demotic, technological, robust, full of bluster, simultaneously naive and cunning. The first half of it was ruled by the newspaper and by the cinema. It was also the time of popular writing, of huge advertisements, of lettering that invaded every nook and cranny, and even wrote the skyline. America wrote big, with new demotic alphabets, in lightbulbs, in neon, in smoke. One could follow the text of twentieth-century America from coast to coast and read it either as a single, long Dada phrase, or as small, interlinked sections of an epic poem. Walker Evans, while concerned in the foreground with the more intelligible narratives of the socius, also pursued this text in all its variations, from modestly scrawled shopkeeper advertisements of the 1930s to the purely abstract graffiti of the 1970s.

In the early 1930s, Evans was fascinated by the self-referential nature of the sign and many of his New York photographs from this period appear to be meditations on the art of photography. The striking impression of his *Sky Webs*, depicting the work of the General Outdoor Advertising Company in Manhattan, is the photographer's delight in abstraction. The layered jumble of Lucky Strike, the partial "Metro-Goldwyn-Mayer," the name of the billboard company, and the REV . . . underneath form a concrete poem. Like Apollinaire's *Caligrammes*, or the later "concrete poetry" constructs, this image is made in conscious opposition to whatever meaning the signs themselves intended to communicate. In addition to the injunction to look at these fragments of language as a picture, the only commentary involved has to do with the evident modernity of the assemblage. Here, Evans makes the same gesture the cubists, at Apollinaire's urging, made toward the Eiffel Tower. They embraced its modernity and praised its beauty at a time when the traditional art critics found it ugly. But where, for the cubists, embracing the Eiffel Tower was a gesture of defiance, for Evans, in modern America, it was merely an acknowledgment. At the same time, to the recently Paris-imbued traveler, it must have been an esthetic gesture, as well as a homecoming.

The literary preoccupation goes in the opposite direction as well. While language itself is turned into an image, other pieces of the landscape are turned into language. The early New York pictures find endless pleasure in uncovering the shapes of anonymous industrial-age artisans, as well as random instances of city life. Letters, grids, scaffolding, fire escapes, windows and window shutters, chains, lunch counters with their repeated shapes of cups, plates, and saucers, rows of people, smokestacks, the Brooklyn Bridge, girders, clotheslines, all become alphabets, a writing "found" by the camera. These are all modern alphabets, mostly vertical and horizontal, but a reader taking pleasure in "seeing pictures in the clouds" might note cuneiform, Babylonian, Coptic, or Cyrillic. It is doubtful whether any of the cabalistic preoccupations of the surrealists had left residual concerns in the young American. He simply uncovered a rich lode of new shapes and was electrified by the genius of America's anonymous workers.

The studious refusal to allow the signs "to speak" may have had something to do with the fact that Walker Evans's father was an advertiser. I might as well commit here the sin of reference that the very soul of Evans's art would have rejected. But one can look at Walker Evans's picturing of signs as a journey along the father's body. His insistent tracking of his father's handiwork was identical to tracking America's unique role in the world: bountiful father-provider. America's signs in their sophistication or awkwardness inscribe the story of a giving, an urging to partake in the constant overproduction of goods. This is what they urge. What they in fact do is another matter. And it may be precisely in exploring the gap between the cheerful optimism of advertising propaganda and the reality of Depression-stricken America that Evans may have found his art. In this sense, he was a Midwestern son of Willy Loman, the archetypal American. There are few women in his pictures. His world is a male, industrial one, close to that of Upton Sinclair, Frank Norris, and Theodore Dreiser.

Evans would have rejected this observation for two reasons: the esthetic purity of modernism demanded a tabula rasa from the artist, and, secondly, his social rectitude, though not strictly socialist, would have maintained that economic conditions were at the root of everyone's oppressed condition, male or female. As a modernist, he might have shrugged off the Midwestern analogy because his New York sophistication was evident. Signage combined the abstract design with the most pedestrian aims; it was both formal and representational. That alone would have been enough to make a claim to art. As an employee of Roosevelt's great WPA project he might have pointed to the leveling effect of poverty which, even in its folkloric glory, had a flattening effect comparable to abstract art.

Three photographs of the early thirties stand out as typical of Evans's art. In one, a sandwich man is advertising photos at 259 Washington Street, with his back turned to the camera. The irony of the art photographer capturing the unaware popular photographer reappears later in his pictures of blind people. Evans was fascinated by the paradox of seeing, by capturing with his eyes for the eyes those who cannot see either their "capture" or the result of it. In this paradox, he seems to have caught the perfect combination of self-reflection and anonymity that haunts so much of his work. The subject of photography, caught in anonymous circumstances, returns also in his pictures of photography studio windows and movie posters. In *The Royal Baking Powder Steps*, the ascending stairs carry their pathetic message into a putative heaven. This is a "founder" picture, both personally for Evans, who composed a perfect geometric abstraction, and for his successors, like Robert Frank and Andy Warhol, who absorbed it. Warhol's *Brillo Pads* are an homage to it. This picture marks also, if one can be neat about it, the end of the luxury of art for Evans, who was soon called to the front lines of photojournalism.

In *Female Pedestrian, New York*, an enduring textual motif makes its appearance: the newspaper. Since the mid-nineteenth century until its approaching demise in our time, the newspaper has been the single most important tool of working American democracy. Its importance cannot be underestimated. It was read by plebes and patricians, it was both a source of news and a prop for public life. Americans read the paper in their homes, at lunch counters, at social gatherings. The newspaper, with its assemblage of news, advertising, cartoons, and gossip, was the very picture of modernity. Powerful commentators, such as H. L. Mencken in the 1920s, could topple the high and mighty from their columns. News might spark riots or cause waves of embarrassment. In the 1930s, as the world began heading toward disaster, the newspaper became the bible of the workingman. Daily, the moments of impending doom came inscribed there in bits and pieces, mixed absurdly with cartoons and advertising. In this photograph, an intelligent and no-nonsense woman (a teacher, perhaps) holds under her arm a folded paper. The beginning of a headline, CI . . . , is visible. The word is most likely *CITY*, and the entire movement of the woman, looking seriously at someone whose words she may be considering, is determined by that paper and what it contains. This *is* the city, locus of conversation, center for news, place to debate the world. Behind her is the newsstand, repeating in blurred outlines the sharp text under her arm. Newspapers make numerous appearances throughout Evans's work. In a handwritten note to the engraver on the margin of a 1941 photograph of two women sharing a newspaper in Florida, Evans wrote: "Can you make the words HOME EDITION legible without retouching?" A decade earlier, legibility may not have been an issue. But consider what news that decade brought Americans: the Wall Street crash, the Great Depression, World War II. Legibility was indeed an issue.

In 1933, Evans went to Cuba to produce a series of photographs to accompany a book by Carleton Beals, a leftist journalist. This book,

WALKER EVANS: *Female Pedestrian, New York*
(J. PAUL GETTY MUSEUM, LOS ANGELES)

The Crime of Cuba, was published in 1933 with thirty-one photographs by Walker Evans. The Beals book was grounded in the socialist ideology that captured nearly all notable American writers and artists of the time. Particularly important to Evans was the scandal accompanying Diego Rivera's mural for Rockefeller Center in New York. The Mexican muralist had included a portrait of Lenin and an idealized Soviet-type worker in his fresco. Rockefeller ordered the mural boarded up. Evans had watched the work in progress and was outraged, along with most New York intellectuals at the time. Rivera's work was in fact a kind of sloganeering: his figures could just as well have been ten-foot red letters on a black background. The calligraphic nature of most social-realist art was a feature of the times. While Evans's attraction to the ideology may have been lukewarm (after all, he had worked on Wall Street and later had a permanent job at *Fortune*, America's premier capitalist publication), he doubtlessly admired *the writing of the Revolution*. This writing, on a huge scale, had evolved directly, via Mayakovski and others, from Russian constructivism. In Cuba, fired up by socialism, Evans set out to photograph the misery inflicted on Cubans by American imperialism. But his camera had a mind of its own. It was drawn, first of all, to the extraordinary faces on Havana streets, to the large crowds, to pushcarts, and then to the movie posters of American movies. He also photographed facades of Havana buildings that spoke to his ongoing textual investigation. These were rich in signification and a lot more human-scaled than the mega-signs of New York. In *Havana Cinema*, a white-shirted black man is looking into the dark doorway of a movie house. On either side of him are movie posters, including *Adios a las armas* (*Farewell to Arms*). In Cuba Evans met Hemingway and the two men became friends. This photograph may well be an homage to his friend, but it is also a picture that insists on the message of the words. The other movies being shown are *El Aguila Blanca* (*The White Eagle*) and *Esclavos de la Tierra* (*Slaves of the Earth*). It is impossible not to read these titles as a haiku history of Cuba. Nor is this the only Cuban picture where the message of the text is not actively suppressed. In *Havana Housefront*, the name of the hotel, Fonda la Fortuna, stand above *Se Admitten Abonados*, which is a kind of guarantee of respectability. This may have been a particularly important message to wealthy Americans who thought of Cuba as their private whorehouse. The old-fashioned, neocolonial writing of this *fonda*'s name, set off by quotation marks, reinforces this message. In the photo *Havana Facade*, three businesses share the space: a beauty salon, a notary public, and Dr. Zatarain, who specializes in *Enfermedades Venereas—Sifilis*. The lettering of Dr. Zatarain's sign is modern for a modern disease. The back end of an automobile is visible, parked by the doctor's. A fruit vendor stands in front of the building. Once more, the messages do not shy away from us. They are meant to be read. In the end, Cubans, despite shots of homeless people and derelicts, appear more at ease than the destitute Americans who absorbed Evans's camera in the next few years. "How could there be a Depression in America when there are so many cars?" This was a question my uncle, who was a photographer in Transylvania, Romania, once asked my father. Well, compared to Romania there may have been a lot of cars in America during the Depression, but without cars one could hardly conceive of America. Henry Ford, who *did* allow Diego Rivera to depict his assembly line at his Detroit Art Institute, had made America dependent on the automobile. Without the car, Americans could not exist. An amount of time equally great to that given over to the care of their souls by innumerable churches was given over by Americans to the care of their cars.

Leveille's Welding Shop in a Massachusetts town gives us a beauty shot of an automobile below the sign. The bare New England street stretches from a tree in the distance to the license plate of the car. Evans photographed a lot of cars, possibly as part of a project echoing Atget's pictures of horse-drawn carriages in Paris. In *White House Garage*, in New York, a truck inside the open door of a garage is framed by all the reverence due a church saint, perhaps Jesus himself. Three men are posing in front of it. The signs read, WHITE HOUSE GARAGE, DAY AND NIGHT PARKING, and PLYMOUTH–SERVICE–DODGE. To the side is another truck, parked deferentially as if awaiting its turn to worship. Above it are other signs for car care, crowded onto the building like icons. This Jesus-truck reappears in different incarnations

WALKER EVANS: *Leveille's Welding Shop*
(J. PAUL GETTY MUSEUM, LOS ANGELES)

throughout Evans's America. At a garage in Atlanta, Georgia, the car parked beneath the CHEROKEE PARTS sign is surrounded by the Os of hanging tires. The tires look as if they would like to form a word, but they can only speak with their formation.

They say: "O O O O," like someone struck by awe.

Depression-age America speaks often through prices. The prices of foods and entertainment are boldly advertised. Cheap movies and dances exert a hypnotic draw. The *Roadside Stand Near Birmingham* boasts of HONEST WEIGHTS, SQUARE DEALINGS. It is a fish store and it appears to burst with bounty. The hand-lettered sign TO DAY RIVER FISH boasts of "CATFISH 20 ¢ TROUT, PERCH 15, DRUM 15, BUFFALO 15,

EEL 20 ¢. Two boys stand in front of the store hefting watermelons. This might look like paradise to a starving Transylvanian of that era, but this is subsistence fishing. All the fish come from the river and they are cheap, it is true, but fifteen cents may be a big deal. This particular photo had a curious echo for me. When I first moved to Louisiana, I drove past a little store in Baton Rouge that bore a sign nearly identical to the one in the Evans photo. I had not yet seen the photo, but said to my companion all the same: "Looks just like a Walker Evans."

There is still plenty of the rural South that looks just like Walker Evans's work. He photographed the rural South on several occasions. He was employed by the Federal Art Project of the Resettlement Administration to document American small town life in 1935. This work took him to Kentucky, Tennessee, Alabama, Mississippi, and Louisiana. Two years later, he photographed flood refugees in Arkansas and Tennessee. In the summer of 1936 he returned with his friend, James Agee, to work on a piece on "cotton tenantry in the United States." The book, *Let Us Now Praise Famous Men*, with thirty-one photographs by Walker Evans, appeared in 1941. The Americans of those days were tired people. But even in their exhaustion, as they stand in front of their stores, or pass time on a wooden bench in front of the barbershop, there is a determined ease in their stance. They are barefoot, their children are ragged, but they are home. Evans did not document the great westward migration of the Dust Bowl, but some of his subjects may have been on the verge of leaving. Their clapboard shacks are bare. The writing that occasionally frames their world is the hand-lettered sign. PLEASE BE QUITE EVERY BODY IS WELCOME, it says, each word scripted differently, above a fireplace in the "cotton room" of a tenant farmer in Hale County, Alabama. A Negro man sits in Vicksburg, Mississippi, beneath a barbershop sign: HAIR CUT 25 ¢ E.C. CLAY BARBERSHOP. These are, recognizably, and classically, Walker Evans photographs, but we are no longer in the strict, formal universe of the New York signage of 1930. Everything in these photos is meant to be seen. And read.

A further literary extension that is, curiously, more photographic than some of his documentary projects is the series Evans shot in 1948 to accompany an extensive profile of Faulkner in *Vogue* magazine. Inspired by passages of the writer's work, Evans shot Mississippi gravestones and sweeps of land with men behind ploughs. The overwhelming emptiness of the land rhymes with the memorial inscriptions on tombstones. The questions asked by this Southern landscape are no longer about people (who seem to have vanished), but about its very raison d'être.

Walker Evans's fascination with writing had a life of its own. He never stopped producing pictures that turned their subjects into script and thus, implicitly, into reflections on art. The *Photographer's Window* in Savannah, Georgia, 1936, features a gallery of a studio photographer's portraits under the window sign STUDIO. What was his interest in these posed people who were, in all respects, the very opposite of how he photographed them? Was he equating his craft with that of the studio photographer, implying that only an excess of intention (the word *STUDIO*) stood between them? Or was he expressing a wariness, an exhaustion much like that of the tired people he saw through his viewer? Clearly, Evans hated to bother people and preferred to shoot them from the back or from above. Perhaps this too is why he liked to shoot the blind. But the shy impulse that made him want to disappear behind the camera is a writerly impulse. Evans used his camera like a typewriter and would have preferred to be alone like a writer.

The apparent paradox is partially explained by the New York subway series, forty of which were collected in the book *Many Are Called* (Houghton-Mifflin, 1966). Evans took pictures of New York subway riders secretly, using a hidden camera. The faces of these New Yorkers of the 1940s reveal a weariness that is no less tragic than that of the cotton farmers of the 1930s. Although these are city people in a public setting, they exist within a near-absolute loneliness. The world, as reflected in the myriad tensions in their eyes and face muscles, is heavily with them. They are better dressed, some of the women are even pretty, but there is no genuine happiness in any of them. Subway riders do not, even now, reveal much tenderness, but looking back on these people one can certainly feel the burden of the times. Black and white is their only possible expression. Dignity and pride, occasionally present, still belong to a monochromatic world. It might be wrong to generalize, but the world seems to have gotten much lighter (and happier) since the advent of color photography. Genuine relief (and better economic times) arrived at the end of the fifties in the Western world. (The communist countries, of course, stayed black and white until the very end of the eighties.) The writing that accompanies these riders is mostly names of stations reflected in the windows. These are anonymous places of egress that suck them back into the anonymity Evans briefly woke them from.

The "masses," that ideology-laden, bottom-heavy notion of the socialist thirties, underwent a thorough examination by Evans's camera. He photographed the "many," both in their public-private spheres and in anonymous quantity. A very clear Marxist picture is the 1946 *Yankee Stadium with Capacity Crowd and Billboards*, in which a throng of fans swarms unconsciously under advertising for Philip Morris, Burma Shave, and others. The capitalism that rules these people's lives is no longer hidden, as in the capitalist conspiracy of earlier times: it's up there for all to see, in the sky, like God. Patriotism and its crowds come in for a share of critical observation by Evans's camera in the early forties. The (uncharacteristically) ironically captioned, *Bridgeport Parade, Bridgeport Women Insist Upon Their Patriotism*, looks straight at three cherubic believers passing by in a flag-adorned car with the sign LOVE OR LEAVE AMERICA. Beneath the obvious flummery, there is pathos. Italians were enemies so Italian-Americans had to overdo it.

For the more private relationship between advertising and the human soul, there is the 1941 *Subway Portrait* of a pensive sailor beneath a Chesterfield ad. But the sailor's private thoughts are no more private than the gaiety of the girl in the Chesterfield ad. The sailor, whatever his thoughts, is part of the great mass of sailors soon to be

WALKER EVANS: *Yankee Stadium, with Capacity Crowds and Billboards*
(J. PAUL GETTY MUSEUM, LOS ANGELES)

leaving for war. He is, in fact, part of a triply anonymous mass: that of soldiers, of subway riders, and of advertising victims. Evans's intuitive grasp of loneliness foreshadowed the alienation central to postwar existentialism. In the 1935 *Interior Detail, West Virginia Coal Miner's House*, a Coca-Cola ad featuring a Santa and a graduation poster stand filled with cheer over an ornate, empty rocker. The human has gone somewhere to look for work: the ads themselves, not what they promise, are his sole possession. The picture vibrates with his recent absence.

Ads themselves, without any humans, came often within the purview of Evans's lens. The 1936 *Show Bill, Demopolis, Alabama* displays a racy ad for the "Silas Green Show" against a brick wall. In it, a (possibly) black man is dancing with a frilly flapper. Evans was keenly aware of the temporality of advertising and thus of a fundamental feature of America: the constancy of change. The ads he photographed looked already nostalgic, though they were brand-new. The movie posters hawking *The Man from Guntown* and *I Hate Women* are eternally lurid though clearly destined for the trash heap. The ephemeral writing of popular entertainment is almost as achingly present as the Southern tombstones with their grander claims at permanence. This is perhaps one of the unintended ironies of photography: the obsolete and the ambitious are equally preserved on film. Not all of Walker Evans's pictures of advertising have the same quality of critique, however. The 1937 *French Cleaners, New York* advertisement is simply a delightful image. Evans photographed it with the kind of care he took in photographing African art earlier, in 1935. It is a typically Evans letter-poem framing an esthetic discovery. Cleaners, clotheslines, and uninhabited dresses make frequent appearances also, a whimsy that he may have caught from the surrealists but which he certainly passed on to his pop successors, like Jim Dine.

Walker Evans's discovery of color came before he actually began using it. His Gulf Coast series, though still black and white, has hints of color in it. The place and its denizens tint these pictures from within. *The Sarasota Municipal Trailer Camp*, with its flower boxes, is a wedge of upcoming fifties American kitsch in full gaudy bloom. Evans photographed the wintering grounds of the Ringling Brothers Circus in Florida, with its carved wagons, elephant "kraal," and lion cage. The atmosphere of wartime Florida is far removed from the Depression. The place is animated by a future of roadside attractions, mass-produced trivia, rivers of baubles, cheap plastic, portable housing, lawn furniture. Once more, Evans's eye discerned within the present the makeup of something yet unborn.

All writing is abstraction that points, paradoxically, toward representation. Evans's early sign photographs point, inversely, toward abstraction. Later, the composition appears to share room with the message. One can look at them as concrete poems or as documents. They work both ways. Walker Evans portrayed America, but he also created Walker Evans's America and, by extension, a Walker Evans text. This poem can be read in any number of ways: chronologically, simultaneously, or randomly. Surprisingly, it is a more coherent poem than *The Bridge*, Hart Crane's anguished lyric, because the tensions of the creator are dissolved in the seeming objectivity of the camera. I say "seeming," because the effort to create just the right distance is written in every picture. Whatever that distance was it became just the right distance for the following generation of photographers. Evans's America became the way to see America and we continue, for the most part, to see it that way. Halfway through this essay, a question came up: would Walker Evans's work have been any different if he had remained solely a New York artist? It's an absurd thought but worth considering these days when art photography, without its utilitarian and documentarian side, has become a métier sufficient unto itself. The loss, it seems to me, would have been incalculable. Which is another way to say that art is art but photography is also the getting out there and catching it. Evans got out there and made his art give the world back to us. His text may then be also a kind of train and bus schedule, or, at least, an admonition to pick up the schedules and head out of town.

PART FOUR

DAVID GRAHAM: *Texaco Boot*
(COURTESY OF THE PHOTOGRAPHER)

The West

It is quite possible, of course, that we blindly passed comfortable stopping-places, but to us that whole vast distance from Omaha to Cheyenne was to be crossed with as little stop-over as possible. Aside from questions of accommodations and speed laws, the interminable distance was in itself an unforgettably wonderful experience. It gave us an impression of the lavish immensity of our country as nothing else could.

—Emily Post, describing a 1915 cross-country motoring trip

California is the Garden of Eden.

—Woody Guthrie

Come visit us again and again. This is a state of excitement. But for heaven's sake, don't come here to live.

—Governor Tom McCall of Oregon, in January 1971

The West, my beloved West, is so utterly different from the South, one could write a treatise on the distinctions. (One will perhaps do one day.) All that is spacially familiar to a creature of the Atlantic Coast (Homo Atlanticus) is upset here by scale. The proportions of land and sky to the human body are changed dramatically. Just like in the old movie Westerns men grew taller, women stronger, children more self-reliant. This enduring cliché has frayed considerably today. Instead, one might say now that men are crushed by their commutes, women join support groups, children drift aimlessly. Still, the energy that moves people up or down is relentless. To speak of cities in the West is to speak of human habitations created for the purpose of maintaining long supply lines. Western cities rise (or clump) not so much for the purposes of containing the land and the sky, but for the exercise of surveying it. Airplanes have obscured the true dimensions of the West, but as any driver, cyclist, or pedestrian knows, the reality of the West humbles humans. I have been in nearly all the bigger Western cities and have felt their common texture of rawhide, desert sand, and ocean salt. Even Seattle, Portland, and San Francisco, poised now on the edge of the future with their space technologies, preserve at their core an essence of rawhide and dust. The psychological pressures that drive Americans elsewhere have greater intensity here, magnified by greater expectations and, consequently, by greater disappointments. The scale, as Henri Poincaré said, is the phenomenon.

I could have chosen cities other than the ones presented here. I could have expanded my thumbnail sketches of San Diego, Sacramento, Reno, Salt Lake City, or Denver, but in the end I reflected mainly on those places, big and small, that I know well. Western cities are home now to new forms of urban thinking because they are changing fast. Immigration, particularly from Latin America and from Asia, is transforming Western communities. Green politics and questions about identity have more urgency here. Still, the landscape of the West remains the dominant fact of lives lived on the other side of the Continental Divide. The descriptions that follow are subject to the vagaries of travel and quirks of timing. Which is not to say that there isn't any narrative: there is, but it's woolly and digressive, like the Rio Grande.

Albuquerque, the Wide Part of the Chile Pepper

The first time I ate a New Mexican green chile pepper it left a hole in my memory shaped exactly like a chile pepper. The only way to fill this hole is to return to New Mexico over and over and have lots of chile peppers. Over the years, I have done just that. I have spent many days in Taos and Santa Fe, ostensibly doing other things, but secretly indulging my appetite for chile. In retrospect, the things I was engaged in all had something to do with the chile even though the connection may have been hidden.

Take, for instance, the World Heavyweight Poetry Championship in Taos, which I attend every year. This festival of poetic pugilism takes place every summer, usually between June 10 and June 14. Poets from all over America head for this quaint little city to test their wits against one another. The bout is a serious event. Poets train strenuously for the contest, while the town falls prey to competitive fever. On the night of the bout, everybody in town turns up, nervously clutching at handicapping literature, which may include reviews of the poets' books, pages torn from reference books, or psychological profiles commissioned secretly by the bigger gamblers. Yes, wagers are placed on the possible winners. The bout consists of ten rounds. Each round is a single poem, with the last round given to improvisation. I was the challenger in 1989 against the two-time undefeated champion Lewis MacAdams, and let me tell you, it was no picnic facing the Los Angeles heavyweight in a room packed full of his supporters. I won almost every round, and ended up beating the champ and taking home the Max, the iron sculpture named after the New Mexico poet Max Finstein. The secret of my success can be told now. Every day I had some form of chile. In the morning, I ate a green chile omelette with blue tortillas on the side. For lunch, I had enchiladas with red chile. For dinner, I had both red and green chile with sopapillas for dessert. It's true, I weighed six hundred pounds by the end of the week, but this was, after all, a heavyweight contest. My opponent, on the other hand, lived on toast and broccoli, due to a weak stomach and a strict vegetarian disposition (stricter than mine, in any case).

Another time, I drove to Santa Fe to shoot a movie about psychics in the area. I met astrologers, channelers, past-life readers, rebirthers, crystal healers, aura fixers, poetry prognosticators, archetype ferreters, and many other kinds of spiritual workers who comprise one of the larger industries in the Santa Fe area. (The others being art, opera, and catering to the idleness of the wealthy.) I submitted myself to the ministrations of many of these gifted people and I found out more things about myself than, in all honesty, I need to know. I mean, I now have such a vast amount of self-knowledge, I can barely move for ennui. I already know what's going to happen about six years in advance. In order to survive these ordeals of self-examination, I secretly left crew and camera behind, and stuffed myself with chile-pepper-based dishes at some of Santa Fe's cheaper restaurants. (These are very hard to find, given the town proclivities for nouvelle cuisine to complement the New Age!) In the end, I survived the psychics and the grueling shooting schedule only because of my secret diet.

Taos and Santa Fe are marvelous parts of New Mexico. Next to the bat caves at Carlsbad and the honky-tonks of Espanola, they are the state's greatest draws. But something still nagged at me, namely that I had never spent any time in Albuquerque, New Mexico's largest city. I always arrived here at the airport, only to be picked up quickly by one of my friends and driven to those bejeweled spots in the mountains. I decided to investigate the mysteries of Albuquerque for its own sake. The city's name, for one, had always intrigued me because it took me years to learn how to write it. I still can barely pronounce it, but at least I don't get lost among its profusion of vowels anymore. The city was named in honor of Don Francisco Fernandez de la Cueva Enriquez, the eighth Duke of Alburquerque (notice the extra r, mercifully dropped in later years). The dukedom of Alburquerque (the name comes from *albus querque* or white oak) still exists in Spain, and the duke personally visits his namesake city in New Mexico every year, just in case the New Mexicans want to give it back to him. It was settled by Spanish pioneers in 1706, which makes it an old and distinguished city, as well as a major trade center for many goods, including the chile pepper, which is the only good that interests me.

My friend Peter Rabbit and his wife, Annie, the founders of the Taos World Heavyweight Poetry Bout, together with the poet Amalio Modueno, picked me up at the airport on this particular visit. Peter and Annie have an apartment in Albuquerque for the winter because it was too cold in Taos for Peter, who has a problem with his knees. The temperature in Albuquerque was a splendid seventy degrees while in Taos the snow was up to the rooftop of their house. Albuquerque's wondrous climate is, incidentally, the reason why people have been migrating here for the past six decades of the century. Nestled between the watermelon-colored Sandia Mountains and the volcanoes on the west mesa, the city has a nearly ideal climate all year round. The Rio Grande River, the fifth largest river in North America, slices the city in two, air-conditioning it when it gets too hot.

In Peter's battered car, which make was impossible to ascertain, having reached that venerable plateau when a car is no longer known by its brand name but by the word *jalopy*, we huffed down Central Avenue, old Route 66, to Garcia's, Peter and Annie's favorite Mexican restaurant. The proximity of chiles made my mouth water, so we talked about the local food. I declared my undying love for the chile, and for Mexican and New Mexican food in general, noting that the only dish I could not abide, even in the days when I ate meat, was menudo. Amalio took immediate offense at this bold assertion. "Garcia's," he declared, "has the best menudo on the continent." "That may be," I said, "but cow stomach floating in fat-globulated broth just doesn't do anything for me."

Garcia's was a simple and cheerful establishment dominated by chile motifs displayed boldly on the walls. The motherly waitress had various kinds of culinary advice to help me navigate the deceptively simple menu. I ordered the enchiladas with chile verde, while my dinner companions had various things, including the "best menudo on the continent," which Amalio ordered to prove a point. I closed my eyes to the chatter of my friends and dove in. The New Mexican chile contains something called 8-Methyl-N-vanillyl-6-nonemide, a substance that is doubtlessly addictive. The active ingredient is a chemical called capsaicin, which makes the chile hot. Its effect on the brain is instantaneous. It begins like a small flame on the tongue, and spreads rapidly through all the extremities of the body, warming it in a peculiar and satisfying manner. The chile is an ancient and honored pepper, supposedly interbred in ancient times with the tomato. It was known to the Aztecs as a war god, used presumably to blind the enemy. They also used it as a means of pedagogical persuasion because I remember seeing a picture of Aztec parents holding a disobedient child over the smoke of burning chile peppers. Luckily, we don't do that anymore, though, in principle, this could be a powerful incentive to learning. The modern version of the chile pepper was developed by Dr. Roy Minoru Nakayama at the New Mexico State

University in the 1950s, and it has the advantage of being mild enough to be eaten by non-Aztecs. Of course, there are various degrees of hotness, on the Nakayama Scale, which rates Bahamian Pepper at ten, Tabasco at eight, and New Mexico at one. I rated Garcia's chile at about seven, as my eyes filled with grateful tears. The enchilada plate, incidentally, was the size of a small European village. I snuck a look at Amalio's menudo, noting with satisfaction that it looked just as gruesome as I remembered. He, however, slurped on, oblivious to criticism. The great shock, not greater than the hotness of the chile, but perhaps equal to it, came when it was time to pay. The bill for four people, for food and two beers apiece, came to $18.61. That's right, eighteen dollars! I don't think you can eat that cheaply in Mexico. Of course, no checks, credit cards, or other such unreliable paper was acceptable. Heck, if everything was still this cheap I would cut up my credit cards in a Mexican minute. (Okay, I know that's politically incorrect, but so is a country mile, and a Romanian omelette.)

After dinner, we met up with some more friends of the Rabbits, all of them eager to show me the true Albuquerque. I had been under the impression that my brief visit might consist of pilgrimages to such well-known sites as the New Mexico Museum of Natural History, or the magnificent Rio Grande Bosque, a stretch of woods right in the middle of the city, or perhaps the renowned Rio Grande Zoological Park where there are more than a thousand animals representing more than three hundred species. But, no. Natives don't care much for tourist attractions. They always want to show you the real city. That was totally okay with me. I do the same thing when people come to New Orleans.

So, instead of heading for the zoo, we drove about an hour and a half through the city, a drive that gave me a sense of just what a huge city Albuquerque is. There are only about half a million people here, but each one must have an acre all to himself. Evening had fallen by then, and the lights came on, giving the impression that we were on a ship sailing between mysterious and massive mountain ranges on either side of us.

Our final destination turned out to be Epi's, a Latino dance bar. Onstage a wild-looking band, led by a one-eyed singer named Hurricane Al, was making the place rock to a mixture of salsa tunes in Spanish and English. The peculiar texture of the songs and their powerful blend of Texas country and Mexican ballads reminded me of the chile pepper. Here it was again, even in the music! Señoritas in long evening gowns, or dressed alluringly in miniskirts and sparkly tights, danced with dark-haired hombres on the big floor in the middle. Peter and Annie, Amalio and Maria, and the rest of our table got up to dance, leaving me to take in the sounds and flavor of the place. I felt somehow that I was in a very exotic locale, somewhere far away. I have been told that this is how people feel when they visit New Orleans, but this was a very different place, with Mexican, Indian, and Anglo accents, a peculiar blend specific to Albuquerque. For the next several songs, my friends tried to make me get up to dance, but I am exceedingly shy in this regard, having danced only a few times and then after only three or more whiskeys. As the pretty waitresses floated by carrying huge margaritas and Bud long necks, I abandoned myself to the music, which spread like a slow fire through the body, exactly like the chile. I saw then that the New Mexican chile was more than a pepper: it was an organ, like the hand or the mouth.

Driving back, I was too busy talking to notice that we had slowed down to a crawl. When I did notice, I looked out the window to see what the traffic jam was all about, and I saw the most extraordinary spectacle. Next to us, behind us and in front of us, a procession of fantastic cars cruised slowly. Some of them were customized four-by-fours, raised high in front and low in the back. Some of them had huge tires and convex-mirror hubcaps that shone like midnight suns. Others had equally giant tires and hubcaps in different shapes, with spokes or rays polished to a brilliant sheen. These vehicles emitted a steady salsa or rap beat as they rocked by, driven by young Chicano men with long hair carefully combed back. Following each one of these "low-riders," as my friends called them, were regular cars filled with girls presumably connected to the men in the shiny chariots. They laughed and called to one another, moving as slowly as if they were the ducal procession of the eighth Duke of Alburquerque. The mile-long stream of cruisers finally turned about a half hour later, leaving us to speed for no good reason on the suddenly darkened next stretch of Central Avenue.

My friends explained that we had had the good fortune to observe one of the city's most colorful rituals: the low-riders' Saturday night cruise. They told me also that this by now traditional cruise was not to everybody's taste. I could see where being in a hurry wouldn't do you much good on Saturday night. The police, responding to the pleas of some of its more harried citizens, apparently tried to enforce speed limits for a while, but threatened by massive civil disobedience, they mercifully eased up. I wasn't in a hurry. Not at all. It was Saturday night, after all, and even if I had been in a hurry there was nothing I could do about it. Certain things are meant to be savored slowly, and certain aspects of Albuquerque culture are definitely better savored that way.

Next morning, we engaged in a different set of activities. It was a beautiful bright morning, the sky the color of blue corn tortillas. We strolled leisurely in the neighborhood of the University of New Mexico, stopping in bookstores and cafés. One of the liveliest literary spots in New Mexico, the Living Batch Bookstore, is as good a book place as you're likely to find anywhere, including New York City. Well disposed toward local culture, it carries poetry and novels by local authors, books on Pueblo Indian people, art books on the rich traditions of the Southwest, and, most important to me, cookbooks on northern Mexican cuisine. I bought about six of these, including *The Best from New Mexico Kitchens*, by Sheila MacNiven Cameron, and then, for form's sake, a novel by New Mexico's senior poet and novelist Rudolfo Anaya, called, appropriately, *Albuquerque*. I immediately sat down to read Ms. Cameron's book because I was already feeling the need for a dose of chile. They have chairs and places to sit and read at the Living Batch, which is the mark of a civilized bookstore.

Later, we had a cappuccino at a place called the Zurich, which was, at first glance, a generic youth café of the sort one might encounter in New York or in London's Soho, but on closer examination, the Zurich offered a red bean, green chile, and corn pizza. Also, along the wall, local art revealed the ubiquitous signs of familiarity with Pueblo symbols. Young people dressed in black, the international uniform of artistic youth, leaned back on their chairs, perusing the latest journals of New Mexican literature while sipping their espressos and biting down on tortilla chips.

I capped the morning with a quick visit to the Maxwell Museum of Anthropology at the University of New Mexico, a small but discerning collection of Southwestern folk art. My favorite local form is sand painting, a ritual art practiced by Pueblo people. Grains of colored sand are drawn together to form vivid symbolic images of religious life. There is something about the fragile, temporary beauty of such work that moves me. All art is more or less fragile and doomed to disintegrate, but there is something about recognizing such fragility right from the start that makes it, paradoxically, durable.

I was feeling pretty fragile myself after the previous night at Epi's, so I spent the rest of the day merely enjoying the dry, warm transparency of the desert air, and chatting with my friends around their kitchen table in the small adobe house they are renting. And I had more chile, of course.

When the time came to leave, I felt nostalgic. I clutched my garland of chile peppers which, Amalio advised, I can just chop up and fry with some eggs, and said my good-byes. I calculated mentally how long the peppers were going to last me. I plan to return for the World Heavyweight Poetry Bout in Taos in June, so I should be okay if I'm careful. Two chiles per day for the next few weeks should bring me right up to the time.

San Francisco

San Francisco has been a consistent provider of trends to our ever-trend-conscious nation. When I moved there in 1970, the city had just finished inventing and (simultaneously) burying the hippies. The Haight-Ashbury neighborhood sported all the scars of the hard-fought war for love and happiness. The winner, sad to say, was neither love nor happiness, but hard-core, street-toughened addiction, which stalked the once-flowery street corners in the form of heroin and amphetamine dealers. But enough hippies still remained to give the place the dreamy air of the love-ins and be-ins, although most communes, head shops, bookstores, and cafés were crashing down hard. In 1970, one could still wear flowers in one's hair, but it was advisable to also carry a can of mace.

There was nothing in this whole country like San Francisco one quarter of a century ago. While the war in Vietnam was growing increasingly uglier, the separate nation of the disaffected young had set up a world with different rules right in the heart of a major American city. If you didn't have any money—and most of the pilgrims reaching the Haight didn't—you could always eat for free at one of the many communal kitchens, or crash at one of the pads that constellated the

143

neighborhood, or get clothes from the Diggers or from the free boxes. There were hippies elsewhere in the world, but the prototype was formed in the city of St. Francis and, like that vegetarian, pigeon-loving saint, the Frisco hippie was filled with innocent (or naive) delight in his magical city on the hills.

The magic of San Francisco, I always thought, was a consequence of the light. I felt blessed to wake up to a bright morning in the Mission District at Twenty-fourth Street near Dolores Park, with the light streaming in my bedroom window. It was as if the whole sky had just come in and surrounded the bed. Down below, people walked their dogs to the park, enveloped in a golden shimmer that was both healing and forgiving. Going out for a doughnut and an espresso, I heard the word balmy a lot. (Croissants hadn't yet conquered the West, it was still a doughnut and toast world!) Most people were really nice, they had a sunny disposition, so to speak, even though Richard Nixon was still president, and the war in Vietnam had just moved to Cambodia, and the Zodiac killer was loose. Some people were so nice in fact that, according to San Francisco's then beloved wit Herb Caen, they caused a four-year drought by constantly telling everyone to "have a nice day."

On an average day, Golden Gate Park, aptly named, was home to ninety-nine varieties of light. I counted them. I will mention a few—you can discover others—the oblique light between eucalyptus leaves at sunrise; the light in the Garden for the Blind, which is set up as a cornucopia for every sense *but* sight: yet here the light does truly magic tricks; the little chunks of colored light that fall on the ground between the light-thin profusion of orchids inside the Golden Gate Conservatory; the light on Hippie Hill in the Panhandle where the first love-in was held (if you squint you can still see eleven thousand naked hippies waving their arms hopefully toward the soon-to-come year 1969); the light-turning-to-cloud in late afternoon as the Pacific breezes drive in the fog. In San Francisco, the light changes with the clouds, from brilliant to foggy gray. When I lived there, the light matched my psychic weather, from cheeriness in the morning to melancholy in the afternoon, but I was never sure if the light followed my moods or my moods followed the light.

The key, I believe, to all the novelties that sprung out of Frisco is the light. The city itself developed because of the California Gold Rush: gold, as everyone knows, is the metal of the sun, par excellence. Gold traps light, it *is* light, and it gilds everything in the city, from the gates of Chinatown to the mighty banking buildings downtown. San Francisco's most famous outlaws, from Black Bart, the gentleman-poet-bandit, to Patty Hearst, the heiress turned bank robber, were after gold. Fire, which is wild light, is San Francisco's most enduring specter, and firemen are among San Francisco's best-loved citizens. Madam Coit raised a phallic tower in honor of her favorite fireman, and today, Coit Tower is the official emblem of the city. The Beat poets and artists gathered around the still extant—and thriving—City Lights Bookstore. The aforementioned hippies were also a creation of the light revealed by the ingestion of LSD-25. As for the city's relatively recent but important gay community, I only need to remind the reader that the original meaning of the word *gay* contains light, in the sense of lightness and play. Light or the lack of it influences the mood of the citizenry and civic decisions. Even some of the city's most notorious murderers have blamed their acts on the absence of the sun.

Given the city's foundation in light, it seems only natural that one of the great cooking trends of our time developed and flourished here: light cooking or nouvelle cuisine. Health fads that are mainstream now have haunted the Northern California coast like a benevolent wind since the late nineteenth century when organic farmers first settled in her fertile valleys. One of the world's famous mystical botanists, Luther Burbank, lived in Santa Rosa, near San Francisco, where he grew new plants, including thornless cactuses, by smiling a lot while talking to them. The California wines that are all the rage now owe their qualities to the light trapped in their grapes.

But—enough nostalgia! What has San Francisco given us *lately*? The California economy is in the doldrums, which means that the good times are somewhat under strain. Many California products, from computer chips to politicians, have lost their luster. Silicon Valley shows signs of wear, while Jerry Brown is doing a liberal radio talk show in the age of Rush. Not exactly the recipe for success. Still, the city that rejected both Charles Manson (who went off to Los Angeles) and Ronald Reagan (who went to Washington) couldn't possibly be out of steam.

My friend Carmen Vigil, who is a keen observer of culture and a true San Franciscan, now lives in Bernal Heights, a mixed Hispanic and white neighborhood near the Mission District. Twenty-five years ago on this hill the only place to have a drink was the Ribeltadvorden, a friendly bar named by its owner after a drunken slurring of the name of his WWII ship, *Liberty and Order*. Now, Bernal Heights has a fair number of neighborhood eateries and taverns, including the Sausage Factory, a Hungarian restaurant run by a bearded Magyar who makes all his own sausages and pastries.

Imre, which was his name, responded in a none-too-friendly way when Carmen introduced me as his Romanian friend. As everybody but Carmen knows, there is no love lost between these two noble mini-races. Nonetheless, we soon established common ground in our mutual love for stuffed cabbage, strudel, and palinka, a fiery liqueur. Imre's pretty young wife nursed her baby while those dishes arrived, and whistled along with the sexy *chardash* pouring out of the tape deck. Not exactly nouvelle cuisine, the stuffed cabbage and strudel were recklessly topped with sour cream, and tasted exactly like my grandmother's. I filled with nostalgia like a sausage skin. I needed a nap.

On the way to the Phoenix Hotel, a lovely oasis in the stormy cesspool of the Tenderloin—a neighborhood dreaded by decent people since the nineteenth century—I saw some extraordinary creatures that moved dreamlike toward us. Not sure whether my nap had begun or not, I asked Carmen if they were real. "They are," he confirmed gravely, "they are the neotribals." They sure were. The gender-nonspecific youths now nearing wore bones in their noses, brass rings in their cheeks, sticks through their lips, and discreet gold rings in their pierced eyelids. "Excuse me," I inquired of the most decorated member of the neotribals, "do you wear such hardware all the time or only when you go out? And tell me, are you the latest, newest thing, the postpierced, posttattooed thing?"

"That's too many questions," he said, with a metallic lisp (he had a silver disk on the inside of his lower lip). "But, yeah, we're like way beyond piercing."

With the help of his fellow tribesmen, he gave me to understand that they didn't even *talk*, let alone mix, with the merely pierced (under eight holes in a row, anyway) or the *slightly* tattooed. Communication was only possible when the wannabe neotribalist was pierced for *bones*, had more than one quarter of his or her body surface covered in tattoos, and was, hopefully, branded. Branding was a sore subject with at least one of the tribespeople who had a huge open wound on her back. It was supposed to look like a star when it healed, but she wouldn't know for sure until then. Sometimes brands took their own paths to form.

The neotribals were not at all shy: one of them turned around to show me the tattoo of a sun enclosing a dragon on the back of her neck. She could never see it, she explained, unless she used the mirror. The tattoo existed mainly for the pleasure of others, who regarded her from behind. The neotribals, I concluded, were not selfish people. And they were definitely new—the newest thing—out of San Francisco.

Felled by Hungarian cabbage and altruistic tattoos, I fell on my futon at the Phoenix and did not rise until supper time. I wasn't exactly hungry, but I'd made a dinner date with Carmen and he was there just before seven P.M. The Phoenix Hotel caters to visiting musicians, so the clerks are extremely knowledgeable about things most ordinary humans don't care about. In the lobby, for instance, they rent art movies, sell massage discount coupons, replace guitar strings, and have a complete listing of performance-art events.

"What's the hippest, newest food in San Francisco?" I asked the desk person.

"To eat?" she said.

"No, to write about," I countered.

"Everybody's eating Caribbean right here at Miss Pearl's Jam Lounge, and it's pretty enough to write about."

We decided to give it a try, although I live in New Orleans and Creole food is no news to me. Miss Pearl's was crowded with trendy young people, though not the latest trend. These Creole food fanciers were barely tattooed, if at all. They were well, if conventionally, dressed, and they had credit cards. No neotribals here, which was too bad because I would have liked to see what they did with their bones and disks while supping.

Miss Pearl specialized in some fine jerked chicken with spicy mango sauce and ham-flavored greens with West Indian curry sauce, which is what Carmen had. I ordered the fish, which turned out to be a hefty mound of filets affixed to a spicy mushroom-and-bread stuffing. It floated on an island of mustard yellow spice. It was not New Orleans but Jamaican Creole, and too sweet for my taste. It was pretty enough to look at, but there was nothing nouvelle about it. The whole thing cried, "I'm fat! Long live pork!"

Carmen explained that the newest thing in San Francisco, not just the food, was indulgence in everything that was supposed to be bad for you. It was a funny thing: after convincing America to eat light and healthy, the capital of granola consciousness turned the tables. The in thing was calories. I didn't find this hard to believe. San Francisco does have a sense of humor. In fact, I think that this "let's eat and do everything bad and then die" trend has already spread to other cities, notably New York, where butter has made a spectacular culinary comeback.

A reggae band struck up in the bar adjacent to the restaurant and the calorie-saturated youth rushed onto the dance floor to do the steps of another generation.

"Is everything retro?" I wondered. "I thought that most retro already came and went. We had the sixties last year, then it was the seventies for about seven months—a short comeback, thank God—and now it's what, the eighties?"

"No," Carmen said, "now it's a combination of everything: a little retro, a little ethnic, a little neo. It goes by neighborhood. The old Haight is almost all sixties now. If you'd pulled a Rip van Winkle in 1967 you'd think nothing changed."

One of the very trendy, though decidedly hush-hush, new phenomena was a store called Good Vibrations in the Mission District. It's a clean, well-lighted place as Hemingway would have liked. The displays were well spaced and spare for leisurely browsing. A middle-aged woman and her daughter were taking turns weighing a hefty object called the Jeff Striker.

"It has the texture and feel of the real thing," the mother explained.

"Of *some* real things," the daughter said doubtfully.

A kindly grandmother with kinky white hair, or perhaps a kinky grandmother with kindly white hair, was studying the hitachi doublehead, which advertised its versatility as perfect for sharing. Meeting the eye of a sympathetic stranger, grandma shook her head at the difficulty of finding just the perfect gift for that special someone. In the end, she settled for a Tiffany smoothie in metallic silver. It was the original and popular seven-and-a-half-inch-long, one-and-a-quarter-inch-thick battery vibrator, available also in blue, pearl, pink, purple, white, and yellow.

Yes, it was lunchtime at Good Vibrations on Valencia Street in San Francisco and the girls were shopping for instruments of pleasure. The tastefully arranged window of this establishment was arrayed with some scary mechanical devices that had procured women pleasure in the dark ages of the past. Some of these rusted *objets* looked like dentists' drills or lunatic restraints. Studying these products of illicit ingenuity one could not help but feel grateful to the pastel-colored silicone stimulators of our time. How can one not prefer the Willie Plug, for instance, or the Jane Wah, or the ever-popular G-spotter plus? And yet, there was something about the cheeriness of this market that was downright eerie, as if it were for aliens rather than humans. Maybe it was the shoppers' determined bravado, or maybe it was the lack of anything dark, dirty, and forbidden. Whatever it was, the place felt oddly asexual, like a hardware store. The Laundromat next door, full of half-dressed, sleepy people, was a lot sexier for some reason.

Next day, I went to the Haight. It was true. Head shops and coffeehouses shined with psychedelic colors. The Cha Cha Cha Café, which was started by a family (commune, for the uninitiated), was still there. Charles Manson's bus was parked at the corner of Haight and Schrader. Panhandlers perfect in every detail staffed the sidewalks. The only difference from the sixties was that nothing was free. The psychedelic posters—especially the vintage ones—were very pricey. And the Cha Cha Cha was now a half block long and it served, er, *nouvelle* Caribbean! Charles Manson's bus was a replica. And the beggars didn't even mention change. "Got five bucks for a croissant and a cappuccino?" one of them asked.

"What happened?" I said. "Inflation?"

"Hey," he said huffily, "I'm not a bum, I'm *homeless!*"

Right.

The Haight, it seemed, was home to many neotribals. They squatted around their *lattés* in the cafés, waiting for the end of the world. The end of the world, flying saucers, divine revelations, and supernatural beings who look just like us seemed very popular. One store window displayed news articles and photos of aliens, as well as a large chart explicating the government conspiracy against UFOs. The New Age was well represented in the form of crystals, tarot cards, palmists, past-life regression coils, and transporters, which looked like huge toy blenders. Some of the peddlers of these things were aliens from the Middle East. Alas.

San Francisco has always had a disproportionate share of believers in strange things. The occult has been commonplace here since the days of Sutter. In my day, people gathered regularly in Golden Gate Park to await the apocalypse. It was fun. I am particularly fond of an episode in the mid-seventies when I was told by a barefoot dreamer that the many agates along the beaches of California were actually precious stones washed out from the sunken palaces of Atlantis.

Dr. Weirde's Wierde Tours: A Guide to Mysterious San Francisco reports a goodly number of sites for the mystically inclined visitor. At the intersection of Haight and Schrader, in addition to the Cha Cha Cha and the faux Manson bus is the Temple of the Sun, which we are told, is where "ten thousand years ago . . . arose the magnificent Atlantean city of Tlamco. . . ." Another Atlantean site in the neighborhood is the stone circle atop Strawberry Hill, which is where the "monks of Atlantis and modern occultists commune with the heavens." The Laguna Honda Reservoir just southwest of Mount Sutro was once "the lake that supplied the Atlantean city (Tlamco) with water via aqueducts."

Dr. Weirde holds nothing back when it comes to weirdness, so I was not surprised to learn that the fabled tunnels under Chinatown may actually be "locations where magical adepts could be 'channeled' or teleported from one spot to another." This is the kind of thing that makes a city fun to live in. Still, I did not want to become distracted from my goal—which was to ferret out new trends—no matter how fascinating other topics might appear to be.

Fisherman's Wharf might strike one as an unlikely place for innovation. A beloved tourist attraction for decades, this waterfront strip of restaurants and T-shirt shops is also home to a number of tour-boat operators and fishing-boat rentals. From here, one can get onboard a boat to Alcatraz Island, its notorious prison outlined like a malignant sketch in the fog. The Rock, as Alcatraz is called, was home to famous criminals, but also to just-plain criminals who became famous after they reached Alcatraz, either because they tried to escape and never made it, or because they became the subjects of movies like *The Bird Man of.* . . . I visited Alcatraz once and spent a horrifying five minutes in the haunted cell 14–D. I could barely imagine what months of confinement here could do when just five minutes brought me to the edge of a sincere scream. No, I had no desire to visit Alcatraz again, but something pulled me here.

There was a drizzle in the air and there were few tourists. Bored gulls scanned the empty piers looking for the odd sourdough crust. I had just finished a shrimp cocktail and had disposed of the wrapper in a lidded trash bin. The gulls made hostile noises: two of them swooped down close to my still-shrimpy fingers and cackled their displeasure. Every fishing boat in the city seemed to be at dock. Some of these vessels were weathered veterans: unpainted, proudly rough, piled high with fishing nets, crusted with barnacles, sporting some old-fashioned gal's names, like Lilly Marlene and Vivian Red. All that was missing was the Jolly Roger flying from their masts, and I am sure that it came up as soon as their captains reached the open sea. Some of these foul firetraps displayed phone numbers on the side, being presumably for hire. I was just imagining what an adventure it might be to actually lease one of these conveyances instead of, let's say, a brand-new cabin cruiser with electronic hoists, when a gnomish gent in a pea coat approached. "Wanna go fishing?"

"Looks like rain," I said.

He scrunched up his face just enough to produce a toothless laugh. "They bite bigger inna rain!"

"Which one's your boat?"

He pointed to the worst of the bunch: a wobbly barque with several missing sections. A kerosene-blackened cabin sat precariously in the center of it. A clothesline sporting the gnome's long johns swayed in the wind, stretched between the cabin's leaning chimney and the mast. "Do you live on there?" I asked.

"The whole family," he said enigmatically.

I thanked him and walked on. Still, I can't help thinking that I missed something that might shortly catch on. Boarding old picturesque wrecks and taking off into the unknown with whole families of mutant fishermen might be the coming thing. Nah.

In further pursuit of the nouveau, I took a bus to the bohemian capital of the West, North Beach. Here, bohemians have put their stamp on everything. Bookstores display signed books, café chairs have been sat on by many famous behinds, and the houses and skyline look familiar from paintings and drawings.

I went to pay my obligatory homage to City Lights Bookstore and its proprietor, the poet Lawrence Ferlinghetti. I found out, to my surprise and delight, that the city of San Francisco had named a street after the poet. What's more, I got a tour from the man himself who walked me to the top of Union Square in North Beach and pointed with evident pride to the small street bearing his name: Via Ferlinghetti. This was nothing short of astonishing. No other city in the world, as far as I know, has ever named a city street after a still-living poet. Ferlinghetti himself had led a successful fight a few years back to have some of the city streets named after distinguished San Francisco writers. Thanks to him, there is now a Jack Kerouac Street, a Kenneth Rexroth Street, a Dashiell Hammett Street. But all those writers are dead!

The sky was very blue over our heads and we were bathed in that special and blessed light that makes San Francisco seem the kindest burg on the planet. Ferlinghetti told me that the old Italian families who lived on Via Ferlinghetti had no idea who he was, but when it was explained to them that he was a poet they posed no obstacle to renaming the street.

Any city that names streets after poets deserves to be saluted. I doffed my hat. This is a very new thing indeed and I can only hope that the rest of America follows suit. I once lived on Melville Street in Baltimore and I was always proud that the city had had the good taste of naming one of its streets after a great writer. Until I found out that the Melville in question had been an obscure state legislator. But just think: Codrescu Street in New Orleans! A real happening place. I'm not ambitious: a nice little side alley off Bourbon Street will do.

Highway One

Out the car window, a bank of clouds rolled up like a scroll over the ocean. A flag stuck on a deserted pier flapped in the stiff breeze. The Pacific was agitated yet calm, a contradiction that applies to all things Californian these days. I was in search of Mendocino, a windy jewelly city set into the flesh of wooded hills on the Northern California coast. But there were no signs for it the entire length of Highway One. Nor was it on the Avis map of Northern California. Was it, I wondered, because Mendocino was known as the Sensimilla Capital of the world and the state didn't want dope tourists? Or was it the Bolinas Syndrome, which caused the inhabitants of that village to rip up any highway signs mentioning the name of the town for fear of messy gawkers?

I used to live close to this coast, in Monte Rio, a small town under the redwoods, ninety miles north of San Francisco. I stopped on the way to Mendocino. I remembered the grocery store, the Pink Elephant Bar, the quonset-hut movie theater, the gentle shabbiness of the locals. But everything was not the same in Monte Rio twenty years later. The Knotty Room Restaurant where our young and enlightened company met for coffee and the greasiest eggs in creation was gone. The Post Office, burned down by a teenage arsonist, had been reconstructed in standard U.S.-issue cinder block. And the bar where my friend Jeffrey Miller had his last drink before crashing into a giant redwood on the way home was now a parking lot. Still, the best thing about the place was intact: the smell, a windy scent of forest moss and river mud, with hints of ocean and wild fennel. This was the main reason I lived here: to get my coffee in the A.M. while filling my lungs with this stuff.

The town had burned down several times in its history, and at least once since I'd lived here. The prosperity that occasionally afflicts California before politicians get hold of it has passed nary the feather of a golden wing over it. Poverty was still the rule here and the winter cords of wood before houses looked solid.

Out of Monte Rio, Highway One seemed designed by a drunken contortionist as it loopdelooped over hills and sheer drops under redwood forests, crossing clouds, sunny pastures, misty forests, and incongruous seaside communities. Some of these communities were old and had a reasonable agreement with the elements, but some were new and defiantly vulnerable. A house that may have been the dream of an architect and a real estate agent pushed off a cliff right over the ocean. Whoever lived in there must have been half dead from the terror of looking every morning over such vast intensity. His cup of coffee must've trembled in his hands when he turned to his equally shaky spouse on the windswept porch to tell her unconvincingly, "For the first time in the whole year since we spent five million on our dream house I couldn't hear the waves in my sleep last night." And she, dropping coffee cup over cliff into sparkling infinity, "I think I should see a psychiatrist five times a week in Los Angeles."

And that, come to think of it, is how California teeters between dream and nightmare, between the land and the politics, the fantasy of the nouveau riche and the steady crouching of the indigent proud. Highway One is the visual representation of all that. I did find Mendocino, but it added little to what I have just written.

Southern California: La Jolla

La Jolla's only resident homeless person committed a grave faux pas. He shuffled past the Birkenstock Shoe Gallery, edged past the three of us sipping cappuccino de jour and dark roast of the day at the outdoor café table, and *dropped a candy wrapper on the sidewalk*! Immediately, as if a long stakeout had just paid off, a young T-shirted employee of the Birkenstock Shoe Gallery streaked out faster than lightning and *picked it up*. She then stood glaring behind the back of the longhaired indigent, shaking her head at what was no doubt a repeat offense. She then strode back in, pleased that once more the sidewalks of La Jolla were safe from litter.

It's that kind of place. Spotlessly clean, bathed in brilliant white light, smelling of ocean and eucalyptus, inhabited by people with perfect bodies, sporting immaculate sidewalks, strewn with dazzling boutiques—a precious little jewel nestled in hills and expensive real estate. Even the homeless person was relatively well groomed by comparison with his equivalent in, let's say, nearby San Diego. He wasn't smelly or gross and he merely mumbled discreetly to himself in an unthreatening manner. The three of us, two New Yorkers and this New Orleanian, were sitting peacefully at the café, enjoying the sweet evening breeze and wondering whether the place was real or not. Especially doubtful were the New Yorkers who are, as a rule, exceptionally suspicious of paradises, particularly if they are in California. After observing the tanned and peaceful locals strolling leisurely, one of them observed: "How come everybody here is either under twenty-five or over seventy-five? What do they do to everybody else?"

It was a fair question. Golden youth possessed of bodies that could have modeled for classical sculpture (or Benetton ads) were everywhere. Long-limbed, blue-eyed, blond young men and women with dazzling white teeth visible in a perpetual smile sauntered past, dressed in loose white shirts and casual shorts. Sprinkled through this limber throng were well-preserved, sporty elders in golf attire, some of them carrying golf clubs (the rest carried shopping bags).

We asked our limo driver, Tiffany, about the mystery. "Oh," she said, "I'm twenty-five and I don't go out much anymore. I used to. Now I like to stay home and look at the ocean!" Tiffany, one of the drivers for the Sheraton North Grande Torrey Pines Hotel where I was luxuriating, had golden hair, blue eyes, and a dazzling smile, and looked to me anywhere between eighteen and twenty-three. Now the mystery had been solved. After you turn twenty-five in La Jolla you retire to your cliff dwelling and contemplate majestic sunsets through the wall-sized plate-glass window. When you get to be seventy-five you come out with your golf clubs and, after a day on the brilliant green of the Torrey Pines Municipal Golf Course, you head for the La Jolla shopping zone where snotty New Yorkers make remarks about you. "How much is a nice house around here?" one of the relentless New Yorkers asked Tiffany. That's another thing about New Yorkers: if they can't find anything very wrong about a place (particularly in California), they immediately conceive the urge to buy a house there. In fact, I have a hunch that a good number of La Jolla's hilltop dwellers are transplanted New Yorkers still looking for a good reason to hate the place.

"Oh, about a million," Tiffany answered casually.

I picked up Coldwell Banker's Showcase of Homes brochure to see for myself. For three million nine hundred and eighty-five thousand dollars, you can pick up a six-bedroom, four-and-a-half-bathroom pad with pool, spa, lawn with rose garden and, of course, a magnificent ocean view. If you aren't quite that well heeled you can try for a modest two-bedroom, two-bath penthouse with fireplace and wet bar (and ocean view) for a mere two hundred and sixty-five thousand. All this sounded perfectly reasonable to me since I can't afford any of it. (Isn't it wonderful how the price is no object when you don't have any money?)

The Sheraton North Grande Torrey Pines was itself a dream palace. Floating on a cliff above the calm blue mirror of the Pacific Ocean, it was a model of service and pleasure. In addition to twenty-four-hour room service, it sported several gardens, a pool, whirlpool, and workout rooms. Perfect youth in green uniforms smiled their by-now-familiar perfect smiles and met your wishes with equanimity, whether you wanted a limo to a nude beach or needed to fax something directly from your computer disk. One of the buttons on my telephone said "Butler." Yes, just like a British aristocrat I had my own butler. This butler shined shoes, brushed your coat, ironed your shirts, polished your cuff links, monitored the number of ice cubes in your cocktail, and shook the beach sand from your shoes. At least this is what I think he did because I couldn't bring myself to actually employ the butler. I'm too modest for such ostentation and, besides, I think that the great thing about America is that we have invented machines to do the work of servants. Nonetheless, I did appreciate the thought, and otherwise took full advantage of the hotel's other amenities.

In the company of the same New Yorkers I went to La Jolla's famous Black's Beach, a nudist stretch of sand where men and women without a stitch of clothing on did things like play volleyball. This, I must say, is a ridiculous undertaking for men, though women look perfectly fine when they whack the ball over the net. The interesting thing about Black's, which was duly noted by one of the New Yorkers, is that the naked people didn't look terribly different from the clothed people on Prospect Street. They seemed to be as unselfconscious at the beach as they were on the street. Furthermore, perfect tans and perfect bodies gave an impression of sameness. To tell the truth, the nudists looked less distinct than clothed La Jollans who already looked pretty much the same to us, barbarians from the East and South. Needless to say, no one in our little group took off any clothes at all, not even shoes, an oddity that was enhanced by the fact that at least two of us wore black from head to foot. Naturally, we attracted more attention than anyone else in paradise, eventually drawing unto ourselves the disgruntled gazes of a dozen naked people. We beat a hasty retreat to our waiting limo and went to Torrey Pines State Beach instead. This was much better. A snaky tongue of fine sand ran along the foamy edge of the Pacific to a huge flat rock, known to the locals as Bathtub Rock. This amazing stone jutting straight into the water looked to me like a giant picnic plate on which should have rested enormous grapes and boulder-sized hunks of cheese. Standing on it, I felt that I was sailing out onto the vast waters. Two enormous fish leapt suddenly into view, vaulting over each other. I had never seen dolphins before, except on PBS, but here they were, playful and magnificent. I watched them until the sun fell into the sea, a flamboyant ball of various hues of orange and red fires. Even the New Yorkers were silenced by the spectacle and they said nothing for nearly two minutes.

Of course, after the sun was almost swallowed by the waters, one of them commented: "This is too much. It's like being in a postcard." But she didn't sound too convinced. She only said it because she remembered that she was a New Yorker and felt that she might be losing her edge. It can happen. We all know someone who went to Southern

California functionally articulate and, within a year or two, has been reduced to saying "Wow," "Awesome," and (in more lucid moments) "Have a nice day."

For the next two days, the little group tried its best to hold on to its tough, world-weary attitude. We went back to the main boutique drag on Prospect Street and thoroughly investigated it. The most interesting establishment was the La Valencia Hotel, an elegant 1920s-vintage building where Greta Garbo used to hang her hat. The Mediterranean Room restaurant here had a kind of solid ambience that even the New Yorkers had to accept. Needless to say, the ocean outside did its mesmerizing best to reduce the group to silence, but it was tougher to do in here, especially after a couple of beers. A plate of huge, juicy shrimp next to a swirl of spicy sauce was so delightful I sank into it, forgetting my table companions for a moment. When I came out of my shrimp trance, I heard one of them say: "How come shrimp get this big in California? Something wrong with their hormones?" Still, there was no way to prove the superiority of Long Island small shrimp over the jumbo California beasts, especially since they were so well cooked. This argument was continued over several meals where shrimps were ordered. At the Torrey Sheraton, the chef did something spectacular to his shrimps, including some very innovative sauces and tangy garnishes. Shrimp after shrimp, La Jolla cuisine proved its consistency. Even the shrimps in the shrimp burrito at a simple food stand on Prospect Street turned out to keep their dignified firmness.

Due to the way I was raised, I'm not big on shopping. My mind goes blank if it has to distinguish more than three different objects at the same time. Dragged against my will into Pilar's Beachwear, I had to suffer the vision of hundreds of swimsuit styles with names such as Too Hot Brazil, Baja Blue, Oscar de la Renta, and so on. The peak of fashion in swimwear, these things still looked to me just like minimal little patches of cloth whose function was to reveal rather than hide.

The New Yorkers complained, of course, because they believed that no one could fit into these things. The boutique guide (who was perfect in La Jolla ways mentioned earlier) pointed out that all sizes were available, from Cs to DDs, whatever that means. And, if still nothing was to be found, one could actually take a quick trip to a Dr. Cook in Coronado and undergo lipo sculpture, a painless fat-sucking process that returned one to the beach (in a Pilar swimsuit) within two days. That was too much even for the New Yorkers who found themselves speechless once more, so we beat a hasty retreat.

About the only objection left after our visual, culinary, and shopping explorations came later that evening when one of the nearly silenced Manhattanites pronounced: "Still, there is nothing *serious* in La Jolla!" She meant things like the Museum of Modern Art and Carnegie Hall. The trouble was that there *were* serious things to be experienced in La Jolla. The enormous campus of the University of California at San Diego houses the Scripps Institution of Oceanography, located on bluffs that overlook the town. This institution, founded at the beginning of the century, is the oldest and largest marine research facility in the United States. Everything you ever want to know about fish can be found out here. Unfortunately, the easy living and constant lazy pleasures of the place had eroded our resolve. Next time, we promised each other, we would do the serious side of things in this paradise. We would visit the Salk Institute, founded by the discoverer of the polio vaccine, and the Scripps Clinic and Research Foundation, a leading center for biochemical research. The university library has one of the largest collections of contemporary poetry—including some of my books—that is being used by scholars from all over the world. And also the newly renovated Museum of Contemporary Art and the D. G. Wills Bookshop.

"That's all good," grumbled one of the you-know-whos, "but how can anyone do research and go to the library when the weather's always perfect and when everybody's at the beach?"

That was a good question. It must take loads of will and dedication to shut oneself inside a dark laboratory or a library when one could be surfing, gliding over the waves in a psychedelic glider, biking down hills to the ocean, stretching on the sand watching perfect examples of one's fellow human beings, sucking megashrimps with half-closed eyes, or simply staring out the window of one's dream aerie. People capable of ignoring such things would have to be tough. Yes, tough. The New Yorkers, who think that they are the only tough people in the world, were very quiet when I made this argument. It was tough enough for any of us just to stay awake amid all the dazzling beauty. Imagine going to work. Impossible.

One of the pleasures of the little town of La Jolla was its proximity to San Diego (some say it's the same city) with its spectacular zoo, museums, and parks. Not very far was Tijuana, where a whole other world of sensations was available. Throughout my brief stay, I kept thinking of all the other things I could have done, but I regretted the most not being able to visit some of the fabulous botanical gardens, estuaries, and lagoons in the area. It would be worth taking a good two weeks out of this busy life to wander about Batiquitos Lagoon, a large wetland that will be completely sedimented in fifty years, the Santa Margarita Estuary with its one-acre nesting island for terns, the Tijuana Estuary, once home to the now endangered clapper rails. The other thing that bothered me, besides the lack of time, was being unable to identify most of the wild varieties of trees, bushes, and grasses around us. I knew the eucalyptus, I was familiar with one or two cacti, two rubbery succulents, and I recognized sage, first by its smell and then by its bushes. I was familiar, of course, with the skinny, tall palm trees that give Southern California such a strange, shimmery quality. And I learned to recognize the Torrey Pines for which all my surroundings were named. But I had no idea what that plant with the velvet soft silvery ears was, or that tree with the pointed deep green leaves that looked like little shovels. That's another reason to come back, plant book in hand.

The New Yorkers were pleased, though they hated to admit it. Before leaving, they had a meeting and swore on the Lexington Avenue IRT not to let themselves be seduced so easily next time.

"I'll admit, some of it is okay," one of them said, "but there is too much *nature* here. And it's too expensive. And everyone's perfect, white, and looks the same in or out of their clothes."

There was something to those last two objections. But the first was nonsense. There is never too much nature. The name *la jolla* comes from the Spanish word *joya,* meaning jewel. One can see the justice of the description, even if it's got some flaws.

Christina of Pasadena

My friend Julian Semilian and I had just been victimized by a lecture about God at Claremont College in California, and were in great need of libation. Disregarding the advice of a local that there wasn't much to be found in Claremont after nine o'clock, we rushed into the desert night of Southern California's urban sprawl looking for wine. While we drove around in Julian's Toyota, we considered the great dangers to the human soul that arise from 1) trivializing God, and 2) the unpeopled desolation out the car window.

The first danger was best expressed by a girl in front of us at the lecture who wrote in her notebook: WHERE IS THE JOY? and JESUS HELP ME—my sentiments exactly. Talk of God should be passionate, if not necessarily joyful, and anyone who had written God's biography ought to have some deep insanity from having to listen to the tapes of the interview over and over. But maybe the man hadn't interviewed God at all.

What was certain was that nobody in this area had interviewed any human beings as to how they preferred to live. Half-built subdivisions sprouted into the desert night, fronted or shadowed by mega-stores in neon-lit malls as empty as the God man's heavens. Not a soul was to be seen on the streets. Finally, after a great weary drive we returned to Claremont and chanced upon a Greek restaurant inside one of those cutesy SoCal malls that looks like badly glued postage stamps about to be blown away any minute by the Santa Ana.

We got our wine and sat reflecting on the consequences of God's abandonment of Californians, when a Mercedes Benz screeched to a halt in front of us, and out of it spilled a slightly disheveled young woman in a fetching miniskirt. "Why, gentlemen," she asked us, plopping down in a seat at our table, "am I so happy?" She had a slight French accent that gave her question, or as it turned out questions, particular poignancy. "Why?" she continued, "do I make everyone happy? Why doesn't anyone hate me? Why don't I have any enemies? I suffer and suffer from happiness. Why?"

To these questions we had no answer, so I commented simply that she could be the Christ of Happiness, who so suffered from it, she became French. Julian asked her her name and she answered simply, "Christina."

Well, there you have it. As she peeled away into the night, after having thoroughly startled us, we were pleased, nay thrilled, that despite urban sprawl and descriptive prose, revelation is still possible in the world. It's in the desert, at the bleakest hour, that God makes Her signs. Our poem to her began:

> *On a faux-Greek restaurant near Pasadena*
> *Alit the Christ of Happiness Christina.*

Portland and Salem

Portland is about the size San Francisco was when Tony Bennett left his heart there. In San Francisco, these days, you're more likely to leave your wallet than your heart: it's expensive and thinks of itself as big. Actually, San Francisco thinks it's as big as New York when Frank Sinatra did it his way. Neither Tony nor Frank has given Portland any words to live by, which is probably just as well. Portland is small, energetic, livable, and has its own singers and panegyrists.

Linda Danielson, who wrote a guidebook to Portland, is a poet. She and Joe Cronin, an Irish poet who also makes his home here, met me at the lovely Heathman Hotel downtown, and took me to the Bridgeport Brewing Company, a microbrewery located in an old warehouse. It was evident as soon as we arrived on its outdoor patio that this was a scene. Tattooed young people, bearded older bohemians, and business types lounged in various rooms, reading books and newspapers. Linda explained that the place specializes in English-style ales, and sure enough, we were soon involved in a complex discussion with the wait staff about which brew to start with. This was a serious conversation, of the kind one might have with the sommelier at Maxim's in Paris, regarding the fine points of different ales and their appropriateness for the early afternoon hour, and the weather. It was drizzling, which is de rigueur for Portland, but the drizzle was light and, by Portland standards, negligible. Joe Cronin explained that the day qualified for splendid, which I didn't dispute. When the sun comes out, he said, the adjective is "magnificent."

Linda decided that nothing less than Portland's very own Firkin beer would do, and sure enough, a pitcher of this native brew appeared. It was very good, but then what do I know? Beer is beer to me and I was glad that my hosts didn't know the abysmal extent of my ignorance. I was nearly killed in Belgium once, when I ordered a Guinness in a tavern. The barkeep lectured me for an hour about the glorious variety of Belgian beers, each one served in its very own chalice. I didn't want to repeat that experience in Portland.

After the first glass, my hosts became expansive. Linda greeted several regulars, and introduced me. A lanky, white-haired gentleman, who looked like Alistair Cooke, told me in his English accent that the day was indeed splendid. One of the establishment's owners, who'd once read one of my books of verse, sent over a complimentary pitcher. Joe Cronin began reciting poetry. Behind us, the hand-pumped beer engines in the main room hummed most charmingly. A benign aura settled over the pub, leading to thoughts of food.

Bistro Montage was located under a bridge in an urban-combat-type zone, except that, like other such places in Portland, it was a style rather than a genuinely threatening environment. A throng of pierced and tattooed kids was clustered in front, waiting to get in. The waiting list, it turned out, was about a foot long. I didn't quite understand the attraction, but Linda assured me that this was a very hip place and that part of the entertainment was the waiting crowd. The food itself was some kind of cheap cajun (this appellation has gone way out of control: anything burnt or over-peppered anywhere in America is now called cajun) and comfort foods like macaroni and cheese. I could see why the starved-looking youth might need comfort food. They looked awfully forlorn.

"Are you people hungry?" I asked an emaciated trio of teenagers whose clothes were so loose they appeared to be floating in them.

"Not really," one of them, a vampire-pale girl, answered. "We just like to watch people stand in line."

When I asked them where they were from, they mentioned a rather affluent neighborhood.

"Ah," said Linda, "your parents ate enough for two generations." They listlessly agreed with that.

We were now joined by three other poets, friends of Linda's and Joe's, and the six of us began the search for another eatery. We ended up at a place called 1201 Club, a cooler-than-cool joint with jazz and cigars. Two young women in evening gowns smoked cigars in a booth so filled with smoke it looked like Berlin in 1926. The high point on the menu was fondue for six and french fries, so that's what we had, after ordering more beer. The fondue was thick and tart and the fries were fat and garlicky, and after that, I was overtaken by a great desire to nap.

The Heathman Hotel is a marvelous engine of old-fashioned style and hospitality. One of Portland's reclaimed hostelries, it sports a lovely art deco bar and a grand dining room. My room, on the tenth floor, had a gorgeous view of the city at night, looking just as a city should: alive, luminous, pulsing, but contained. There was none of the electric vastness of Los Angeles here or the ostentatious energy spills of New York or Las Vegas. I could even see some stars, and I felt the phantom weight of the mountains in the distance.

Next morning was cloudy, but I had a feeling about it. I was willing to wager that it wouldn't rain, a foolish bet in this city where, according to Linda, the devil won't take anybody because "they are too wet to burn." But something told me that this day might be an exception. I bought flowers and a newspaper in a park near the hotel, and sat down on some steps to watch the natives at play. It was a weekend, so there were families with children and dogs, running around a fountain. A pretty girl came up to me and asked, "Mind if I ask you a few questions?"

"Shoot," I said. "Make 'em personal."

"When is the last time you had a haircut?"

"A month ago," I said. "Do I look like I need one?"

"No. What's the first thing you noticed about me?"

I'm a polite guy. "Your eyes," I said. "Why are you asking all these questions?"

"I'm learning to be a survey taker."

I gave her a flower and wished her good luck.

Jeff and Linda Tross took me me out for lunch. We went to Jake's, a seafood restaurant specializing in Jake's famous crawfish. I live in New Orleans so I feel that all other crawfish have no right to claim anything, especially not fame. But Jake's was home to a lot more than crawfish. The handlebar-mustachioed waiter, who looked like Black Bart, recommended several varieties of salmon, Pacific tuna, halibut, and sturgeon. This was more like it. I'd never had sturgeon, a huge fish that is, in all respects, the opposite of the puny crawfish. The waiter explained that it was a winter-spring fish and this was the perfect time for it. I was about to order it, but Jeff had questions.

"It's not the cheeks, is it?"

Black Bart assured him that Jake's fillet was the choicest cut of sturgeon, no cheeks. I didn't even know that fish had cheeks, but when something's as big as a sturgeon it has everything, I guess, maybe shoulders even. In any case, the sturgeon, cooked with the lightest hand, was superb. The Trosses had salmon with herbs, and declared themselves satisfied. Jake's is an old establishment (SINCE 1892, claimed the menu), and it was utterly cozy. The walls displayed paintings of volcanoes and other Northeast landscapes.

Jeff is a city planner attorney and Linda is an artist, so lunch conversation entailed Oregon, land use, Portland, volcanoes, painting, sculpture, and (inevitably) the weather. The state of Oregon is way ahead of other states in the thoughtfulness it has given to the uses of land. While other places, like my own Louisiana, have barely begun to think about suburban sprawl, indiscriminate building, proliferation of malls, and urban planning, Oregon has already put in place some of the strictest rules in the country. The environment is closely monitored to insure that farmland is used for farming, wilderness stays wilderness, and cities achieve their potential.

Jeff waxed positively poetic about former governor Tom McCall, who had taken aggressive action to insure that Portlandians and Oregonians preserve their resources. He rescued Oregon's beaches from federal highways, and threw a green belt around Portland. McCall was a maverick Republican, who was simultaneously a fierce environmentalist and a visionary. Oregon has produced other such paradoxical characters: Senator Mark Hatfield springs to mind right away. Jeff said that the current governor, John A. Kitzhaber, a Democrat who likes to dress in blue jeans and cowboy boots, shows every sign of following in the footsteps of his larger-than-life predecessors. After dinner, Jeff presented me with *Fire at Eden's Gate*, a biography of Tom McCall. I said that I'd like to meet the new governor and, to my astonishment, Jeff said that he'd see what he could do.

After the sturgeon at Jake's, a walk was in order, so we took a stroll, punctuated by Jeff's informal commentary. And then, the sun put on one of its rare appearances, and I wished I had made a bet. My hosts were convinced that I had some sort of magic power. In the

sunshine, the view was breathtaking. The snowcapped mountains ring-
ing the city rose out of the ground like giant stone mushrooms.

Cuddled between the Cascade Mountain Range and the Pacific
Coast Range in a lush, green valley, Portland is blessed with a wondrous
scenic setting. The Willamette River flows right through the center of
the city, spanned by a number of gracious, pedestrian-friendly bridges.

The Willamette-Greenway Project, initiated by the farsighted governor, Tom McCall, rings the river with parks and recreation areas.
These days when so many urban downtowns are deserted after sunset,
Portland has been reclaiming downtown buildings for use by artists,
craftsmen, florists, espresso stands, renovated old hotels, galleries, restaurants, and nightclubs. A light-rail system, the MAX (Metropolitan
Area Express) connects Portland's historical neighborhoods with the
heart of the city.

Portland is a city of readers: The rain, no doubt, has something to do
with it, but it rains in New Orleans, too, and we don't have Powell's
City of Books. The largest independent bookstore in the country, Powell's takes up an entire block and stocks one million titles. I wandered
inside for about three hours, until I got to Anne Hughes's Coffee Room,
which was filled with coffee drinkers reading books and magazines. It
was a motley crowd. Two gentlemen who clearly did not belong to the
same social set were reading computer books. One of them was poured
into a neat business suit, while the other had a shaved head and a
metal stud in his chin. I fantasized briefly that one of them was a
banker, reading to improve his computerized security, while the other
was a hacker, hoping to crack the other's security code. Or it may have
been the other way around: it's hard to make assumptions about people
in Portland. A fashionably dressed young woman was reading an an-
thology of erotic short stories, while a grungy hipster was reading a

fashion magazine. I was told over and over that Portlandians are un-conventional. That seemed to be the case.

Powell's is famous for its authors' readings, too. Publishers invari-ably send their authors to Portland, but there are quite a few local writers. Gerald Burns, one of America's finest poets, lives here. Winner of the National Poetry Award, he is a gentle and sometimes not-so-gentle adviser to a number of younger poets.* There is also a poetry slam scene of which Linda Danielson and Joe Cronin are part, a rowdy, poetry performance activity that takes place in coffeehouses and pubs around the city.

Jeff Tross came through; we were going to meet Governor Kitz-haber. Jeff never asked once why I wanted to meet the governor, but I felt obliged to explain. "I collect governors," I said. "I've met eight of them so far. I rate them by the firmness of the handshake."

On the drive up to Salem, Jeff pointed out rich farmlands and praised Oregon onions and strawberries with the flair of a poet. In addition to traditional farmers, Oregon boasts some decidedly nontra-ditional ones, like the Russian Old Believers, who settled here. The Believers live communally and dexterously raise what they need for borscht.

Oregon's reputation for tolerance is still intact, though bruised by the occasional cult scandal. A guru named Rajneesh and his orange-clad followers self-destructed in the 1980s after coming into conflict with the local authorities. Even Heaven's Gate, the UFO cult, is thought to have originated in the state. I can see what attracts the otherworldy types. Peaceful as it is, Oregon is situated among some of nature's most wondrous elements. The eruption of Mount Saint Helens was one of our century's most dramatic manifestations. One year, I went

---

*Gerald Burns died on August 10, 1997, shortly after this book was finished.

to the Shakespeare festival in the little city of Ashland, near the California border. In the town square is a little fountain from which flows lithia water, a substance reputed to induce feelings of well-being. From Ashland, one can see Mount Shasta, which, I was told by a native, is a landing pad for UFOs. Not far from Ashland, there is a spot renowned for inexplicable magnetic disturbances that provoke the nauseating illusion of walking up on a downslope.

Salem was not Ashland, though, but a solid, conservative American town, home to the State Capitol. Inside the government building, there are murals depicting the Lewis and Clark expedition and the subsequent history of the state. The legislature was in session, and the building buzzed with lobbyists, tourists, and politicians.

Governor John A. Kitzhaber was indeed clad in blue jeans and cowboy boots and had an engaging and folksy manner. In civilian life, he'd been an emergency room surgeon, and there was something both reassuring and efficient about him. His handshake was firm but not crushing, and he got right down to business when I asked him what was the greatest challenge faced by the state.

"Land use. We are dealing with the pressures of development and increased population."

I suggested that more people can be a good thing and advised him to bring in a thousand Romanian chefs. "The food is good, Governor, but you can use some variety."

Without issuing an immediate executive order to bring in the Romanian chefs, he praised the restaurants of New Orleans, mentioning Commander's Palace, also one of my favorites (Creole, not Romanian).

I praised Jake's in turn, and asked about Salem restaurants.

"There are a lot of places to eat, nowhere to dine."

The governor was certainly going out on a limb.

Our conversation went back and forth between serious issues, such as "encouraging people to live and do business in Portland near the

MAX lines," and the wonders of fresh fish and the magic of cooking
it. I was quite charmed. He gave me an inscribed copy of the *Oregon
Blue Book*, and I said I'd take him out to dinner if he came to New
Orleans.

The Oregon capitol building, like the governor, exuded a democratic, open feeling, devoid of artifice and the trappings of power. The
lack of ceremony was Western, which is something that, I like to believe, is still redolent of the frontier, of raw people power.

Next morning, the newspaper was full of the news of the suicide
of the members of the Heaven's Gate cult. I felt infinitely sad. Another
naive utopia dating approximately from my youth had succumbed to
the harshness of aging and reality. I noticed an old-fashioned barbershop with a barber pole in front, and decided to get a buzz cut, in
melancholy solidarity with the dead utopia-travelers. Inside, the two
barbers were busy cropping the heads of two frowning boys who'd been
brought in by their dad for their monthly shearing. When the barber
was finished, one of the boys asked dad: "Dad, do you like it?" Dad,
who was dressed in clean farmer overalls, looked at the top of the kid's
head for what seemed to me like a very long time, an eternity perhaps,
and said: "A little more off the top."

When my turn finally came, the no-nonsense barber gave me a no-
nonsense haircut and I felt that I was, somehow, in the presence of
genuine America. I looked nostalgically in the mirror at the five-dollar
job, brushed a few hairs off my collar, and walked out into the brisk
air of the Pacific Northwest. It was drizzling, of course.

While I was checking out of the hotel, the operator came out of
the back and said: "You have a phone call." It was a producer at
National Public Radio in Washington, D.C.

"This may mean nothing, but we have someone on the phone in
Romania. The Heaven's Gate Web page was mirrored through a Romanian site."

The NPR producer connected me to a man inside some office in Bucharest, who said sleepily: "I don't know what this is all about."

"I don't either," I said. "Are you a mirror for Heaven's Gate?"

"Call in the morning," he said, "I'm only the night watchman."

It was drizzling in Salem, it was night in Romania, and somewhere over our heads the souls of dead cultists swirled toward the Hale-Bopp comet, visible to the naked eye. The top of my head felt cold.

Park City, Utah: Sundance

I'm a word man, through and through, and it's a solitary profession. When you write, it's just you and your word processor and whatever crowds your head and needs getting out. I don't appear in society very often and then it takes me five Jim Beams on the rocks before I look as if I'm enjoying myself. All that came to an abrupt end when I allowed myself to be persuaded to come out of my cave and write and star in a *movie*. The result, *Road Scholar*, is a feature-length documentary about strange Americans, directed by Roger Weisberg and shot by Jean de Segonzac. The movie took six months to make, and it's a pretty nifty vision of the strangeness and beauty of this land, but it nearly drove me insane. Working together with six people instead of just a keyboard was such a strain on my nature I briefly considered entering a monastery. The only thing that stopped me was the thought of dinnertime at the abbey, which is communal. Even though they are silent, monks are still a crowd, and they make the most awful chewing sounds when they munch that dry bread.

After *Road Scholar* was finished I would have gladly returned to my ascetic ways, but movies are not like books, they need to be *promoted*. After some arm twisting, Roger Weisberg convinced me to go to the

Sundance Film Festival in Park City, Utah. He called it "the American Cannes," fully counting on the kind of glamorous image of pleasure that moniker evoked. He didn't stress the difference, of course, which is that Cannes, France, is on a beach full of topless starlets, while Park City, Utah, is high up in the mountains where snow can be found until July. The Sundance Film Institute and the Sundance Film Festival were founded by Robert Redford, a lover of mountains, skiing, and movies, who combined his passions in a unique combination of resort and movie-lovers mecca. The Film Institute is in Sundance proper, which is Redford's exclusive development some forty-five minutes' drive from Park City. The Film Festival, a yearly event, is in Park City, a small town which, in addition to hosting film buffs for a couple of weeks, is beloved of skiers, retired plastic surgeons, and other wealthy health nuts with money to burn.

Roger said that my presence at this important event was vital to the well-being of our movie, which was entered in the documentary film competition. Winning an award would give us so much prestige and would attract so many distributors that America would soon have no choice but to watch us on her shopping mall screens until we all (Roger, Jean, and me) rolled in the money. Now I'm not adverse to this idea because I always thought it would be rather nifty to own a log cabin above Taos, New Mexico, with a hot tub and a plate-glass-window view of the Sangre de Cristo Mountains.

"Okay," I said. I carefully packed the only sweater I own—a black one—a pair of rugged socks and a pair of heavy boots left over from when I used to live in the frigid climate of Baltimore, Maryland. I know, I know, that's not supposed to be frigid, but I live in New Orleans now and the sight of a snowflake can send me scurrying under the comforter. As I packed, I regarded mournfully the camellia petals falling on my veranda, and asked myself why for the tenth time. Because, came the inevitable reply, I want that hot tub.

Going from below sea level to several thousand feet above can woefully affect constitutions stronger than mine. My suffering began straight away—at the Salt Lake City Airport. It was the *sight* of the mountains that did it. Okay, I'm exaggerating. But I did begin to feel ill when I found myself in a small van, jammed into the core of a gaggle of cheerful folk, half of whom were skiers and half of whom were . . . movie fanatics. Some were both. We kept climbing higher and higher into snowbound canyons while my van companions introduced one another and exchanged business cards with one hand, while holding on to their skis with the other. Everyone asked me what I did, and like a fool, I told them. "I made a movie," I said.

Well, that was the beginning. They festooned me with cards, then they asked me every intimate question even a psychiatrist would think twice about. "Where do you live?" "How old are you?" "Is this your first movie?" It had begun. Schmoozing. For the rest of the week, schmoozing, like the endless snow, rolled over me in waves, squashing and stripping me. It's a wonder I've lived to tell the story.

Park City is a pretty pop-up town that looks as if it has sprung from a Christmas book. The main street, where the festival headquarters—Z Place—were, was strung with precious little shops filled with vaguely Native American art made by contemporary artists, haute couture skiing gear, fashionable sweaters, coats and hats woven from either politically correct fibers or PC-incorrect wolf and mink. There were also a number of eateries where one could dine on a variety of seafood, from mountain trout to New England lobster—flown every day into the SLO airport—prepared nouvelle, filleted à la sushi, or touched with sauces by brilliant young cooks. I got to know these eateries and the fish well, because my schmoozing took place in these establishments where reservations were harder to get than even movie tickets.

Movie tickets to all the movies, including mine, were sold out well before I arrived. The festival staff, a bunch of young, articulate, endlessly tolerant volunteers, set aside a few tickets for me. They were also kind enough to put me up in a condo with a Jacuzzi and a view of the mountains very similar to the one for whose sake I was undertaking this solitude-imperiling journey. I want to thank especially Erika Herrmann and Lois Vossen, without whom this movie could not have been made. I mean, without whom these words could not have been written. I watched Erika and Lois stand firm in a sea of malcontent filmmakers complaining about their roommates, the placement of their posters, and their lives in general, without flinching. These are the kinds of women who settled the West.

I was among the malcontents. Not complaining, mind you, because it's not in my nature, but wondering just how I was supposed to get to my condo, which was up an icy path about two miles from the bright lights of Main Street. I did figure out, eventually, that shuttles were running pretty well, and that almost everyone would give you rides if you asked.

Once I figured out how to get there, I set about the business at hand. My director, Roger Weisberg, who had come up a couple of days earlier to ski, reported that the crowds were loving *Road Scholar*, and that there was "a good buzz about it." For the next seven days I would hear about this buzz whenever I met a new person, which was at the frequency of two per minute. I think this movie-referring buzz is the original Buzz Word.

At the first screening of *Road Scholar* I attended at one of the numerous movie theaters about town, the crowd really did seem to enjoy itself. At least there were no catcalls. Afterward, in the lobby, a group of health-beaming youths mobbed me with inane questions, so I began to glow. I was a s-t-a-a-r. You have to say this just right. At the party—the *first* party—following the screening, I met some *real* movie stars though, which tended to dim the glow a bit. There was Margaux Hemingway, surrounded by grinning admirers, looking exactly the way she did on-screen except *shorter*. I confessed this discovery to our cinematographer, Jean de Segonzac, who pooh-poohed it. "She's *exactly* the same size she's on the screen," he said. Kevin Kline went by holding a smoked salmon and avocado roll, and a woman next to me said: "He can be so good-looking!" I looked, but he seemed to me to be pretty good-looking right at that moment, so I wasn't sure what she meant. My glow was restored when a lovely hand with fingers generously extended—clearly belonging to a star—grazed my shoulders and commanded my attention. "It's *you*," the lovely voice attached shrieked. "It is *really* you! *Fuck me!*" (These last two words do not literally mean what they seem to mean: they are used in Hollywood now to mean great astonishment, so great that the person pronouncing them feels that only the activity so described would render the situation believable. *You* know what I mean.) "I *loved* your movie! You were fantastic! So objective! So dry! So deadpan! So accurate!" That was undoubtedly me. My admirer was Sally Kirkland in an ankle-length fur coat. I entertained briefly the fantasy that she wore nothing under it.

"I'm a big fan of yours!" I confessed enthusiastically, seeking all the while to remember a movie she'd been in. *Any* movie. I came up with *Cold Feet*, a terrific picture that played at the art theater in my neighborhood for about two days.

Graciously, she let me off the hook by telling me to see the *many* movies she'd made since.

For the next few days, I wandered like a black-clad ghost through the snow, from movie to movie and party to party, listening for the distant buzz that would eventually grow into a hot-tub-producing award. I met all kinds of fascinating humans, some of them not even movie stars. One of the festival organizers introduced me to a serious-looking man who asked me how I liked Park City.

"Reminds me of a nineteenth-century Swiss sanatorium where they sent Nietzsche and Kafka for the cure," I said.

"Thanks," he said, "I developed most of it."

Ooops.

That wasn't the only faux pas. I made dozens of them, including a couple of literal ones on the ice. I fell facedown and got five bruises. Everywhere I went, producers kept pitching movies at me without even asking what I did. One woman asked me what I thought about a guy who comes from the future via TV to save the earth. I told her I needed a drink. After the tenth person asked me what my next film project was going to be, I started telling them. "My next project," I said, "is called Eternal Christmas. It takes place in Park City where it's Christmas year-round; everyone who missed it can come here and get a full shot, obnoxious relatives and all."

"Great idea," she said, reaching for her gold-nibbed Parker. The next person who asked found out that my next movie project was called *The Last Fuck,* an incredibly poignant theme of interest to anyone who a) just broke up with a lover, b) is old, c) just found out he is HIV-positive. I didn't mean to be flippant, but the man just walked away from me, not a glance at his Parker.

Well, can't win them all.

As time went by, I began to feel like an old hand. I slid down the icy path from my condo to the Z place coffeehouse where I listened for the buzz about *Road Scholar.* There were thirteen movies in the documentary competition, but the only buzz I cared about concerned mine. I then shook hands with people I'd met at last night's nine parties, whose cards formed a stiff wall in the inside pocket of my jacket, but whose names I had difficulty recalling. After several minutes of schmoozing, I caught the shuttle to the screening of a competing documentary. I was moved, enthralled, disgusted, and depressed by turns. The documentary films were pretty good. Heck, some of them were downright *great.* And they all had a buzz. I sat in the audience, enjoying the picture and wishing that I wasn't in the competition.

As soon as the movie was over, I headed for the next party, usually in the enlightened company of my director, Roger, who was becoming increasingly agitated as the days went by, and the unflappable Jean, who met every contingency with a bon mot. I elbowed my way like an old pro to the silver caviar dishes and scooped some casually onto my toast triangle as if I'd spent my whole life in a Bavarian *schloss* just like the one we were in. I even casually tossed some of my fish egg to the horse-sized Saint Bernard with the whiskey jug around his neck who strolled splendidly aloof among the glittering schmoozers.

We carefully checked the buzz after each of our screenings. Each one buzzed—with a lone exception. One time, when we arrived at the theater, there was a body in the lobby. Someone had fainted and paramedics were at work. A body in the lobby is not a great sign, but it got worse inside. The sound was terrible and you couldn't hear a word I said. And there were two jurors in the audience. That's two out of four.

Toward the end of the week, things became more serious. Fresh copies of *Variety*, which arrived every day, were snatched up before they could be properly unpacked. A new breed of people appeared, fresh from Los Angeles, roaming around like sharks. These were the Plan B people, popularly known as "the killer bees": publicists, agents, and lawyers. Unlike filmmakers, actors, or skiers, these types carried checkbooks and contracts. Shivers went up the collective spine when rumors that *El Mariachi*, a movie made for seven thousand dollars, got a six-million-dollar remake contract. The day the killer bees arrived, a stray bee buzzed me in my condo when I got up. I caught him and put him under a glass. Before I left the place, I thought to release him to freedom, so I threw him out in the snow. I looked for him in the morning. He was dead. Bad sign.

On Saturday afternoon came the long-awaited award ceremonies. Z place was filled to the rafters with everyone either connected to the dozens of pictures in the dramatic and documentary competitions, or hoping to be connected with them. Directors, actors, producers, agents, and movie critics sat close together in wooden chairs looking up to a small podium. If the outside world existed there was no hint of it in here. I hadn't read a newspaper in five days. I had no idea where the new wars were taking place. It didn't matter. This was as bad as any war.

The man himself, Robert Redford, addressed the festivalgoers and wished everyone good luck. The presenter, Seymour Cassel, a performer in last year's winning dramatic film, started out with a few jokes. I snuck a look at the jury, sitting right up front like four bowling pins in an alley full of heavy eyeballs. They looked very serious. Not good. *Road Scholar* is a funny movie.

And then: the winners. As each one was announced, it became clear to me that all the chosen movies were serious ones, just like the jurors. On my right, Jean looked amused. I couldn't see Roger, but I could feel his vibrations all across the room. He was fit to be tied, as they say.

We didn't win, but people said really wonderful things to me. My condo roommate, Victor Nuñez (whose dramatic film *Ruby in Paradise* did win) said: "You need this prize like a billionaire needs a hundred bucks." My sentiments, exactly.

Tired, over-schmoozed, caviarized, and suffering from a condition known as cinematic eyelids (where you see movies on the inside of your eyelids from two to eight weeks), I returned home from the snows to the delicate wafting of my camellia blossoms. I locked the doors. I wrote this from my room where no human being has been able to enter lo these many weeks.

Las Vegas

The first time I went to Las Vegas they had the sheriff escort me and two other poets out of town. We were there to teach poetry to children in Nevada high schools. One of our poems had a "bad" word in it and a teacher complained. I made a passionate defense of poetry, liberty, and street language. The teacher called the principal, the principal called the Arts Council (our employer), and someone called Senator Bible. Senator Bible called the sheriff. The year was 1972, Nixon was president, the Vietnam War was raging, and prostitution was legal in Nevada. Elvis was king of the town, having made his famous comeback a few years earlier. Howard Hughes was still growing his hair and nails in his aerie above the Desert Inn. But poets couldn't say "bad words."

The night before the day we had been told to leave, we picked up two hitchhikers named Happy Jack and Good-Time Charlie. It turned out that Happy Jack and Good-Time Charlie had also been told to scram by the sheriff. It was hard to hitch a ride out of Vegas at night and, since they were both broke, we offered them the floor of our suite. For the rest of the night, the two adventurers regaled us with their amazing Vegas adventures. At one point, they had tried to rob a hotel safe with liquid nitrogen. That scheme, along with some equally spectacular others, failed. So here they were, in the same boat with a bunch of banished poets.

I was sorry to have to go. We had been put up at the Tropicana Hotel. The drinks were cheap. The food was great and practically free. The cocktail waitresses had outfits that would have roused the ire of every sheriff in New England. I didn't gamble much, but my first time out at a blackjack table I made fifty dollars. And where else can you meet two characters like Happy Jack and Good-Time Charlie?

I also liked the drive we took that night to look at all the crisp fantasy of electric color carved into the pure desert air. Tom Wolfe, in

DAVID GRAHAM: *Victory, Caesar's Palace*
(COURTESY OF THE PHOTOGRAPHER)

his classic essay on Vegas ("Las Vegas? [What?] [Can't hear you! Too Noisy] Las Vegas!!!"), tried to give names to the styles of some of these amazing signs. He came up with Boomerang Modern, Palette Curvilinear, Flash Gordon Ming-Alert Spiral, McDonald's Hamburger Parabola, Mint Casino Elliptical, Miami Beach Kidney. As for the colors, most of which do not exist anywhere outside the Vegas skyline, he thought of methyl green, cyanic blue, tesselated bronze, hospital-fruit-basket orange, among others.

The second time I came to Vegas was in 1978, alone this time, and just for fun. My friend Lamar, who lives there, took me on his own personal tour of the skyline. He drove down a dark street and told me to close my eyes. When he told me to open them I nearly went blind: we were on Fremont Street, or the Neon Gulch, the old section of Vegas, built before the Strip.

We parked in front of Binion's Horseshoe Casino, one of Vegas's old-fashioned gambling parlors. Every year, the World Championships of Poker take place here. I had heard all about this fantastic event, with its attendant legends. I knew about the fabled contest between Nick the Greek and Johnny Moss, the gambler from Texas. A million dollars changed hands before the whole bundle passed over to Nick the Greek. The Greek was reputed to have once won sixty million dollars from Arnold Rothstein, the biggest gambler on the East Coast.

My luck, however, wasn't in that class. I lost fifty dollars quicker than you can say horseshoe, and then dropped another fifty dollars for good measure. That was a good thing because now, free of financial burdens (and finances), I could enjoy the unique sin-laced air of the Gulch. There was, for instance, "Nudes on Ice & Steak: $9.95." We didn't go in and I regret it to this day. The place is gone.

Other carnivalesque old places are gone too, but what remains of Fremont Street, aka the Gulch, is now being put under an electric canopy to preserve its historical character.

History, like everything else, moves fast in Vegas. There was mostly desert here until 1946 when a mobster named Bugsy Siegel opened the Flamingo on Christmas Day. Bugsy's vision of a city in the desert took root, though Bugsy himself was killed by his associates when the Flamingo had a less-than-successful opening. After the Flamingo came the Thunderbird in 1948, the Desert Inn, the Riviera, the Dunes. After that came the sixties and Frank Sinatra, Dean Martin, Wayne Newton, Barbra Streisand, Tom Jones, and Elvis. Las Vegas became, in a short two decades, the place where middle-class America could go to enjoy all the stuff that good sense and the church forbade at home. It was legal to gamble and to wench, it was okay to stay up all night (since, inside the casinos, you couldn't tell the difference between day and night anyway), and you could be a glutton and a drunk. Provided, of course, that you were financially solvent and didn't make *too much* of a nuisance of yourself, such as using "bad words" or being unpatriotic.

One thing about Las Vegas is that, no matter how outlandish your appetites might be, they are fine so long as you respect America. After all, the town was the American dream of some first- and second-generation immigrants: Bugsy Siegel, Meyer Lansky, Lucky Luciano. These men knew that, as Bob Dylan sang, "If you live outside the law you must be honest." Or at least patriotic.

One of the strangest forms that patriotism ever took was the all-night celebrations in the early 1950s in honor of the atomic blasts at the nearby nuclear proving grounds. The atomic explosions were usually scheduled for dawn so casino patrons waited up all night, drinking, singing, and gambling. Special drinks were invented for these parties and there was even a Bomb Hairdo worn by some of the Atom Party Gals. When the explosion came, the town rattled, the ground shook, the flash was blinding, and the Las Vegans cheered. Aboveground testing was soon banned by treaty.

———

Over the years, I took infrequent trips to Las Vegas. Each time I gambled a little more and lost a lot more. One time, I went there with a film crew to shoot a documentary for WGBH Boston about odds. We were standing in front of a row of slot machines and I was telling the camera about my mother, who loves slot machines. A woman turned around as I was saying this and she looked a lot like my mother. I asked her to play the machine next to me and gave her ten quarters. I hoped that she would lend some authenticity to my story but, unfortunately, I could never get it out because every time I started to open my mouth, she won and the clinking coins made a huge racket. Finally, I had to give her another ten quarters *not to play.*

On another occasion, I was making another documentary film for PBS, and I came to Vegas to play poker with some of the world's best poker players. This memorable event took place at Bob Stupak's Vegas World, an extravant needle-topped, spaceship-decorated hotel casino. Stupak himself was a legendary Vegas character who was often quoted for tactless remarks and who had once run for mayor and punched out his opponent on live TV. The card dealers at Vegas World wore little bow ties that said: BOB STUPAK. HE'S POLISH.

Stupak was Polish, pugnacious, and quite friendly. He gave the crew and me a short but colorful lesson on odds, poker, and life. And then I sat down to play for the camera with the likes of Tank Top Tony and his father. There was a pile of black hundred-dollar chips on the table. Every time the camera was on, I won. I amassed almost the whole ten grand before the camera was turned off. Alas. As soon as I wasn't in the spotlight anymore, I lost it all. It was a good thing that it was only play money, thanks to Mr. Stupak's generosity. If it had been real money I'd have sweated bullets.

During that trip, I investigated briefly Las Vegas's wedding industry, too. I watched several weddings at the Little White Chapel, and a drive-in wedding. The drive-in took three minutes, cost twenty-five dollars, and the happily married couple zoomed off into the desert sunset. One of the locals told me, "As long as you have a driver's license and cash Vegas is yours. It's an adolescent fantasy world for adults."

But instant weddings and Nudes on Ice aside, Las Vegas was changing. New, more spectacular casino hotels kept rising on the Strip in the eighties and nineties and the skyline became even more fantastic. Egypt's Luxor and medieval Camelot met in the sky without any apparent conflict. Disney cartoons and New York streets hovered equally at ease over the mobs of vacationers from middle America. At the same time, the town kept growing bigger and bigger. The overwhelming sense of controlled naughtiness that was Vegas's chief product kept receding to give way to an almost wholesome image of a town on the go. Not a town on the go-go, but a city going places, a city with bookstores, a public radio station (KNPR Las Vegas), and restaurants without slot machines. There were also changes in the ethnic composition of the place because of the many Hispanic and Asian immigrants who brought with them new flavors and tastes.

The image makers of Vegas, who must be at least as numerous as lawyers, started pushing Vegas as a family-oriented entertainment. But despite the veneer of respectability, the main business of Vegas is still gambling. But as gambling is now being legalized to balance state budgets all over the nation, Las Vegas has to look elsewhere for revenues. Why not, then, make it a family-oriented entertainment center?

Now, gambling is a sin, condemned not just by every church, but also by good sense. You can't gamble to win and the fun is kind of limited after you lose your first roll of quarters. It is said that the gambling industry in Vegas is clean now, a far cry from the days of the mobsters. That may be, but the legalization of gambling in, let's say, New Orleans, brought back rather vividly those mobster days. There has been scandal after scandal attendant to this business, a sordid story of small and large corruption involving cops, lawyers, and politicians.

How can family entertainment flourish in this morass? Can something as ethically suspect as gambling provide family values in an age when the disintegration of the American family is on everybody's mind?

I thought to look at these questions.

A seven-year-old girl with a fat tear glistening in the corner of her eye held on tightly to her fourteen-year-old brother's hand. They were sitting on the edge of a fountain in the huge Arcade Mall at the MGM Grand, waiting for mom and dad. The time was midnight. The arcades were closed. A sign overhead said: YOUTH ACTIVITIES CENTER. CASH MACHINE. The Youth Activities Center was closed. But the cash machine blinked happily open.

Straight ahead was the (closed) entrance to the MGM Grand Adventures Theme Park where the kids had spent the day having fun at the Grand Canyon Rapids, watching two pirate ships fight, going deep into the Haunted Mine, and Going Over the Edge on a huge slide. They had visited a New York street, an Asian village, a French street, and a Salem waterfront. It had been as good (and as exhausting) as Disneyland.

Now they were bone-tired and didn't too much like looking at the open food counters nearby, which were serving long lines of somewhat unsteady people, impatiently twirling poker chips between their fingers. There was the Hamada Orient Express where trays of tired noodles congealed around syrupy asparagus and uncurled shrimp; Mamma Il-ardo's Pizzeria where teens in baggy pants were cracking jokes with the pizza girls; Nathan's Famous where the hot dogs looked as if they'd been scared limp; and Burger King, the true King of America (though Tom Jones, who was the headlining act, might have contested the title).

Mainly, the kids kept staring in the direction of the open maw of clinking and shouting that was the gate to the casino. They had been in there earlier, watching the stiff backs of tense cardplayers and ogling the scantily clad cocktail waitresses, but chances were that if they went there now they would be lost. The throngs milling there looked dense and impenetrable. Mostly they looked the same: vacant faces shining with glee, liquor, and colored light. They had little time or patience for children. It was an adult playground.

Suddenly, a remarkable couple appeared. A bride and groom, married earlier at the Central Park Wedding Chapel, stepped into view. The bride was swinging a magnum of champagne while the groom drank from one of her slippers. They took their places in line at Nathan's Famous. She wanted a chili dog with everything. He just wanted some fries.

"Look," the little girl's brother said, "a bride! When you grow up you can come here and get married!"

That day was not far off, if they could only wait long enough. The little girl was still crying, but her brother was starting to feel positively old.

To get to the slot machines and poker tables you could go through Oz, but Oz was closed now. All there was was the casino. That's where mom and dad, who had no idea what time it was, were. They had said that they would meet the children at midnight, but here was midnight and, if the two previous nights were any indication, mom and dad would be very late *again*. But eventually they would come, mom complaining about her sore arm that had pulled down the slot machines thousands of times, and dad drunk, and broke. It was a good thing, mom later said, that dad left all his credit cards at home in Normal, Illinois, and that the hotel room and the Grand Adventures were prepaid.

Some other kids didn't have it so good, mom said. Their parents left them standing there on the fountain, waiting all night. In the morning, when Oz opened, these kids went up the yellow brick road in Oz and craned their necks around the animatronic figures of Dorothy, the Scarecrow, and the Cowardly Lion to see if they could catch a glimpse of their vanished parents. But once inside Oz, nothing looked familiar. The sky over Oz changed suddenly, too, going from blue to cloudy ominous to lightning, thunder, and rain.

Mom liked to tell horrible stories to scare the children. But at least she came back. Better scared than alone and lost in Oz. The next day, they would all start again early, go to Circus Circus where the kids could play all sorts of games and win everything from stuffed animals to electronic games. And after that, they could go to the Guinness World of Records Museum and Gift Shop, and to the Liberace Museum (which might be a bit over their heads). And after that, if they were still standing, they could take a nap and make plans to meet mom and dad at midnight.

Besides being a place for lost children, Oz could well serve as a metaphor for the new Las Vegas. The MGM Grand, where I stayed, is said to be the largest hotel in the world. At least that's what I was told by the lost boy before his mom and dad came back: "The largest . . . five thousand and five rooms!"

He was impressed. I was impressed. We were making the most out of it. Still, there were more things for me to do than for him. He had the Grand Adventures, Oz, Circus Circus, the Guinness World of Records, Ice Cream, and Hot Dogs. I had slots, poker, keno, sportsbook, booze, Tom Jones, call girls, cash machines, checks, credit, and cigarette smoke thick enough to choke me. His Vegas was like a brand-new fragile skin wrapped around an old, blinking demon.

The twenty-fourth floor where my room was had a pillar decorated with romantic movie scenes of the Old South. If I followed the hallway directly opposite Scarlett O'Hara and Clark Gable dancing on the veranda of a moonlit Tara, and walked about a mile, I arrived at my room. I felt as lost as a little child in Oz when I went up the wrong way and realized it only very late when I ran into security guards es-

DAVID GRAHAM: *Two Women*
(COURTESY OF THE PHOTOGRAPHER)

corting a little man with a black bag full of cash out of one of the suites. A leggy blonde in a spandex suit followed him. That wasn't my turf. I had no suite, no bag, no guards, and no blonde. But I could have. I was an adult.

One great thing about the MGM was the free exercise it threw in. There was nowhere I could reach without a vigorous heart-pumping hike. This was a far cry from the days of old when fat men with cigars didn't like either fresh air or undue strain and preferred their steaks well fried, their mashed potatoes amply buttered, and their desserts creamy.

Leaving the MGM was an adventure in itself, involving finding the exit (not easy with Oz in the way), weaving through complex family groups waiting for their complimentary rides to the airport (prepaid, thank God!), sprinting past taxis, minibuses, and tour buses. The MGM lobby alone was the size of an airport in a midsized city.

On the Strip, some of old Las Vegas was doing business. T-shirt vendors hawked some colorful and naughty wear. I was handed a yellow flier advertising GIANT ½ POUND HAMBURGER: $1.95. On the back it said, FREE COMBINATION: UNLOCK IT & WIN 5,000. I wasn't sure where this combination was: inside the giant hamburger? What was it a combination of? Numbers? A few steps later, someone handed me a brochure advertising PRIVATE DANCERS. The girls within, named Miko, T. J. Farm Girl, Sandra, and Tia, made the best of their endowments. They, like everything else in Vegas, were but a phone call away.

Well, that was more like it. But as I went past the Aladdin Hotel and Casino with its fairy-tale decor, I thought again of the children. They would probably enjoy this fanciful display of virtual arabesque. I would have gone on, but someone handed me another flier that said FREE! FREE! It turned out that a pair of dice and a free pull on "every Aladdin machine" was mine for the taking. I went in and got my free pull (lost) and the dice.

I had despaired of finding any substantial evidence of the much-touted family place that Vegas had become. It was true that families were coming in droves, but was this any good for families or was this just another pretext for letting adults be "bad" at the expense of children? Americans are very good at doing what they want and then justifying it all on some high moral ground. "It was good for the children, honey. They had a lot of fun!" Yeah, and we lost their college tuition.

Still, real families do live in Vegas. And some of them manage to ignore the din, the clanking, the shrillness of the gambling business. Later that night, I wrenched myself from the smoke-filled gaming tables and went to a bookstore. It was a huge place, with enough floor space to be a gaming hall, and it was well attended. There were even kids running around in the children's book section, or sitting on the floor, reading. The bookstore had a T-shirt that said: "Why Gamble Anywhere Else?" and under that was a picture of books that looked like a deck of cards.

Maybe so. But if you have a choice, take the kids to their grandma's. The iced tea's better and her stories actually *mean* something.

PART FIVE

DAVID GRAHAM: *Silos*
(COURTESY OF THE PHOTOGRAPHER)

The Middle

I stop longest
in the flattest, most solitary space:
out in the middle
of the Middle West.

—Freya Manfred, "American Roads"

    In the spring of '27, something bright and alien flashed across the sky. A young Minnesotan who seemed to have had nothing to do with his generation did a heroic thing, and for a moment people set down their glasses in country clubs and speak-easies and thought of their old best dreams. Maybe there was a way out by flying, maybe our restless blood could find frontiers in the illimitable air. But by that time we were all pretty well committed, and the Jazz Age continued; we would all have one more.

—F. Scott Fitzgerald, "Echoes of the Jazz Age" (1931)

Detroit just lies there
like the head of a dog on a platter.

—Jim Gustafson, "Tales of Virtue & Transformation" (1987)

The middle of America where middle Americans live is no different in many respects from the rest of the country. It is, in fact, *more* like the rest of the country. When I first came to this country, in 1966, I lived in Detroit next door to the house where Charles Lindbergh was born, in a neighborhood that turned into a slum, and then burned in the riots of 1967. It was in Detroit that years later, in 1996, my poet friend Jim Gustafson died of poverty and the madness of his city. Detroit gave me both joy and sorrow. I have also spent a good deal of time in Ann Arbor and Kalamazoo, Michigan, decidedly less dramatic places. In Wisconsin I have visited Milwaukee, Madison, and Lake Elkhart. In Illinois, I lived briefly in Chicago and I spent time in Normal, Glencoe, and Carbondale. I have been to Minneapolis over twenty times, and I have swum in the Mississippi River at Winona, Minnesota, not far from the river's source. There are possibly dozens of other places in the vast territory known as the Midwest where parts of my life lie scattered.

I like the Midwest and its people. They are, for the most part, steady, hardworking, honest, and generous. I learned my English there, was married there (to a Michigan girl), and I remember fondly both the industrial grit of Detroit and the pastoral wonder of winter in the northern reaches. I have also written extensively about my youth in the Midwest in the books *Road Scholar,* which contains "Detroit Love Song," and in the early autobiographical books entitled *The Life and Times of an Involuntary Genius* and *In America's Shoes.*

I will not repeat here what I have written in a different light, in different circumstances, years ago. The reader can look those things up. I have chosen the two pieces included here to underline the essentially American quality of the region, and its universality. Books have always been part of the everyday life of Midwesterners in towns big and small, but never as much as today. In writing about the new zeitgeist of books in this region, I tried to illustrate a certain contemporary dynamic. The shorter piece is intended to illustrate humorously the perennial question of roots, which in the Midwest has some surrealistic poignancy.

Books: In Search of the Zeitgeist

I first observed this phenomenon at Kramerbooks in Washington, D.C. It was about ten P.M., and the bookstore was full of snazzily clad young men and women. Some guys were holding books as if they were power tools, not quite sure where you plugged them in. I had just begun wondering if these folks had all been eighty-six'd from a disco, when I heard someone ask: "This book's kinda expensive. Would you like to co-own it?" The asker was a silk-shirted, dress-jeaned man in his early thirties. The askee was a casually tailored, casually coiffed redhead in her late twenties. The book was a first novel by a prison writer.

"Maybe," she said.

Since then, the bookstore encounter has caught fire. No longer happy with smoky singles' bars, alcohol, and voices straining to be heard above electronic buzzing, young adults are finding bookstores perfect for the mating game. I had a book tour coming up, so I thought I'd look into it. I wasn't interested so much in the ritual per se, but in whether there was a whole slew of new readers out there. I wanted to know what kind of books they read to impress each other. Maybe they were discussing my very own book and finding it just the thing to magnetize them. And then I'd be rich, you see.

Revisiting Kramerbooks on a Friday night, I found it much as I remembered it, only more crowded. The crowd of bureaucrats-by-day, debonair-about-towners-by-night jostled one another with thin volumes of hyper-hip fiction. The little bar at the left was jammed with amaretto and cappuccino-swilling wits who commented in mock whispers about the various *chasseurs* with their manicured fingers between pages. The atmosphere reminded me of a little bar in Rome, on Via Veneto. But that had been a venal Via Veneto bar, not an American bookstore in the nation's capital.

"Pardon me," I asked the owner of a lavender scarf with Andy Warhol's name on it, "has anyone ever written anything as conducive to seasickness as Rimbaud in his 'Drunken Boat'?"

I had addressed her thus because in her ungloved piano-long fingers she held the Wallace Fowlie translation of Arthur Rimbaud's poetry.

"Buzz off, buster," she said.

Granted, I was not nearly as dashing as the gym-polished studs who held their latest Word Perfect manuals like bricks, but I could sure turn a phrase. Maybe books weren't what this thing was about at all. Next time I go to Kramer's, I'll try to buy a book. And have the avocado salad in the restaurant.

Library Limited, a bookstore in St. Louis, had a singles' night featuring a mystery writer, Michael Kahn. Two hundred and fifty people showed up and acted out the characters in his book, *Firm Ambitions*. The group created its own ending to the book and also decided how the villain should die. Refreshed after this literary killing, former strangers then took each other to more intimate places.

I liked the idea. I wanted strangers to act out characters in *my* book too.

Nancy Higgins, Library Limited's manager, sounded doubtful. Other singles' nights had featured authors who wrote on relationships, people like Susan Page, and Sharyn Wolf, author of *Guerrilla Dating Tactics*. They'd also had a Literary Pictionary Night, which had attracted a goodly number to the wine and cheese soirees. I thought about this. My book, alas, was about ideas. Those might be kind of hard to act out. Singles' nights at Library Limited began in January 1993 and were held once every month. They are "the place to be" in St. Louis. Nancy attributed their success to the fact that her bookstore provided a "nonthreatening environment" for singles tired or wary of the bar scene. The bookstore made it easy for people to hold conversations and play social games. It also took the spotlight off the self by providing topics for discussions and a framework for meeting.

"Why wouldn't philosophical essays attract singles and make it easier to talk?" I hopefully tried again.

Once again, Nancy didn't think so. In fact, she didn't even know if singles' nights increased book sales or not. "Are they shopping or just meeting?" she asked philosophically, and then answered her own question: "They might pick up a cookbook. Anyway, it's good for the store. It lets people know we are here."

I asked her if the clientele was for the most part young professionals.

"No, it's people of all ages, from thirty to sixty-four, and usually more women than men. This is how it is most places now. . . ."

This surprised me. At Kramerbooks, everyone had been young. But why should that be the norm? Come to think of it, bookstores are even better suited for more mature people looking to meet someone. For one thing, older people used to read more, so they'd have more to talk about. They also used to read better books before television shortened our attention span by the exact inverse ratio that medicine lengthened our life span. It's okay, go ahead, read that sentence again. (And then act it out.)

Not all book peddlers were happy with the idea of their establishments becoming intellectual dance parlors. The manager of Rizzoli in Chicago became terribly defensive when I asked whether socializing of any kind goes on in his bookstore.

"Not encouraged," he said. "We don't serve coffee. You buy books here." He admitted, however, that the Rizzoli branch in Oak Brook,

Illinois, did serve coffee and encouraged conversation. "They have an espresso bar," he added mournfully, as if speaking of a fallen sister.

When I asked him to give me his name, he said primly, "I would rather not."

Okay, God forbid I should quote something. The manager of the Rizzoli in Oak Brook, however, denied vehemently the possibility that people might meet each other in front of *his* shelves for any purpose other than weighing severe ideas in black and white.

"You mean," I asked in disbelief, "that the manager of your sister store is inaccurate in describing masses of caffeinated strangers roaming the alleys holding books upside down while trying to pick each other up?"

"Well, no, but maybe, once in a while," he admitted reluctantly, "someone will linger over a book of nude photographs and sneak a look around. . . ."

He didn't give me his name either. Pressed for others who might allow their *biblio sacrosanctums* to be used for congress, he told me that the Barnes & Noble in Oak Brook was one such shameless establishment. That would be the competition, you understand.

The Rizzoli managers reminded me of some of my old bosses at the Eighth Street Bookstore in New York, in the late sixties. The Eighth Street was very highbrow, a strictly whispering place where any kind of loudness was immediately censured by the arched eyebrows of us young guardians of high culture and three-dollar-an-hour clerks. Still, despite our best snide stare-downs, people managed to make furtive contact even in front of such high-minded sections as Military Strategy and Architecture. I remember in particular, a dwarfish character named Richard, an expressively ugly man who somehow managed to engage stunning young women in conversation. He would stand right up to the cover of Heidegger's *Being and Time*, which one of these frightening beauties would be holding in her marmoreally intelligent hands, and say something that caused her to drop Heidegger and follow him out of the store. I never could hear what it was he said, no matter how hard I strained. It was some sort of voodoo.

Those days are a far cry from the coffeehouses in the well-lit, friendly bookstores of today. Back then, everything was furtive and a little dirty.

At the Barnes & Noble store in Oak Brook, which had been exposed by Rizzoli, I hit pay dirt right from the start. Manager Linda Kurtz loved to talk. She told me that the store opened in November 1992, and the café was up and running by June 1993.

I looked around. There were chairs and tables in the store where people sat reading and writing. A young man and woman who, evidently, did not know each other were holding identical copies of the latest issue of *Exquisite Corpse: A Journal of Books & Ideas*. That *was* amazing! I barely restrained myself from going over and introducing myself. I am the editor of *Exquisite Corpse: A Journal of Books & Ideas*.

What kept me back was the thought that I might be able to overhear their comments about the magazine when they finally did speak to each other.

Alas, it was not to be. A tragic-looking young man with black ebony-frame glasses plucked the female reader of the *Corpse* out of her chair. After she was abducted, the other reader slammed down his copy as if it and not the tragic young man had been responsible for the disappearance of his intellectual twin. So that's how it is, I thought bitterly to myself. Unaware of the extraordinary drama that had just taken place, Linda told me that meeting your date in a bookstore is as common now in big American cities as it was in Paris in the 1920s.

"Well, heck, it's better than Paris!" she enthused. "One hundred and fifty people showed up here last Wednesday for Open Mike."

This is an event that features poets and musicians who sign up to perform. There is even a singles' organization, called Selective Singles, that advises its members to show up for Open Mike.

"People stayed until closing and then they went to places that stay open later. . . . There were eighty people here at closing time last night. People are tired of loud bars, drinking, and driving. They'd rather play charades, talk books," said Linda. "And it's better than E-mail encounters, where you don't see the other person at all. They might be lying about more than just their sophisticated reading tastes."

Not all Barnes & Nobles were created equal. The manager at the Evanston store, who will be known here only as Leslie, began to tremble in fear when I mentioned the subject of my research.

"I am new here," she begged, "I've only been here two months. . . ." In her plaintive notes, I detected someone caught in the horns of a moral dilemma. She knew only too well what went on. But, she didn't think it was *right*! I had caught my first book puritan, someone who didn't think that books and flesh should mix.

"There will be another manager here, coming from vacation in a couple of weeks. I'm sure *she* knows," Leslie pleaded.

Right. I smelled cold sweat: what if the word got out that someone about to buy *The Joy of Sex* actually met someone looking at the same book? And then, perhaps, the unthinkable happened: lecture à deux? And all on Leslie's watch!

I spared Leslie the terror of further questioning, though it had been on the tip of my tongue to ask her just what kind of book she believed would facilitate an encounter. Hypothetically.

I asked others instead.

Mary Sue Glosser, a teacher at the the Art Institute of Chicago who recently had been waiting for her date at Rizzoli in Oak Brook, told me that "guys like to stock up on computer books so that they might impress someone with their seriousness. Women go for philosophy and poetry." She herself was insistently gazed upon, although she held nothing more than the *Collected Poems of Frank O'Hara* in her hands. Her conclusion: "People pick each other up on the basis of the books they are pretending to read."

The bookstore where *I* was reading and signing books, Barbara's Bookstore in Chicago, on North Wells, was a warmly lit place, smelling of fresh wood and new books. It was overflowing with my fans so I couldn't see if it sheltered a coffeehouse or not. In any case, it probably didn't need to, since it is located in Old Town, a part of Chicago that abounds in coffeehouses, bars, and restaurants. Years ago, when I was a poor poet without any fans, I delivered pizzas in Old Town for a place called Luigi's. Barbara's Bookstore stands at just about the place where Luigi's used to be. Goes to show you something. I'm not sure what. Maybe how America's changed: there are books now where pizza used to be. Or maybe that Americans are on a diet now and books are better for your figure than pizza.

Kathleen Gerard, my gracious hostess, maneuvered me skillfully behind the restless mob waiting to tear off my clothes. I told her what I thought my fans might do to me, and she laughed. "That's not a joke," she said. "We had a book signing here with Johnny Rotten, formerly of the punk group, The Sex Pistols. One thousand people with four-foot mohawks showed up!"

Now, that was exciting. "Did they tear things up? Steal books? Spit on people?" I asked.

"Oh, no," she said, "they were all very nice. Johnny Rotten was very nice, too."

What's this world coming to when even Rotten is nice? Goes to show you even better how America's changed. First, bookstores are now what singles' bars used to be. Second, books are replacing pizza. Third, punk rockers write books. Fourth, their fans are nice.

I was confused. I had set out to try to find out what books lonely people read and if my book was among them. I was finding out, instead, that books were only a pretext, like asking someone in a bar what time it is used to be. Still, they are better for your liver, are they not?

I stepped onstage at Barbara's and the crowd went wild. There was polite applause and even a few coughs. I read them some of my essays.

Strangers eyed each other. I could see it happening already. They would wait until I was gone, then discuss my prose, fall madly in love, live happily ever after. And it would be all my doing. After the reading, I asked Kathleen if Barbara's was a hot spot for singles. "I don't think so," she said. "There isn't much room."

I looked around. It was true. Empty of fans, Barbara's was just a bookstore, shelves full of books. To tell you the truth, this is how I like my bookstores. I may be old-fashioned, but it bugs me to see people sitting around looking intellectual. On the other hand, I must be an old curmudgeon. When I was young, I would have loved to go into a place that served cheap, strong coffee, where I could read books I couldn't afford. And if, glancing up from some page of particularly dense poetry with fog on my eyeglasses, I would glimpse a lovely girl equally moved by something even more esoteric, why, I would have been in heaven!

Of course, the coffee isn't cheap in the bookstore cafés. It isn't even called coffee: it's espresso or *latte*, and it doesn't come small or large anymore, but "tall" and "largo." And the coffee jerk is called a *barrista*. And the misty-eyed youth isn't reading *my* book. Gimme a break!

Clearly, I'm of two minds about this business, just as there are two kinds of bookstores. Or maybe there is only one kind of bookstore and there are two ways of looking at it. One is that it's a temple of high culture and that customers are actually pilgrims come to seek salvation. The other is that people with actual bodies, as well as minds, find each other almost as, if not more, interesting than the books they share a liking for. The former type of bookstore hearkens back to the lending libraries of the nineteenth century where hushed decorum was deemed inviolate. It was part of the high-collar Victorian conception of culture. The other type of bookstore, conceived naturally in the frivolous yet intellectually challenging city of Paris, functioned as a place to stimulate thought rather than stifle it. Big American cities in the nineties are getting to be more like Paris in the twenties than London in the 1890s. And it's a good thing, too. I think.

Little Egypt

I had a gig at Southern Illinois University in Carbondale, a place I knew nothing about, so I put out some feelers and came up with this, by E-mail, from a friend: "Carbondale, Illinois, is known as the belly-dancer capital of the world." Now, I know about this "capital of the world" fetish: I used to live at one time between the garlic and the artichoke capitals of the world. You can imagine how proud we looked and smelled. So when Professor Rick Williams picked me up at the miniscule airport in Marion, I naturally asked about these belly dancers. There was some awkwardness. "It's true," the professor said, "that this area is known as Little Egypt." He explained that all of Southern Illinois was known by that name, and that the school mascot of Southern was the saluki, a rare Egyptian dog. In addition, we were near the towns of Cairo, where the Ohio goes into the Mississippi, and the towns of Karnak, Thebes, Goshen, and Dongola. But he wouldn't touch those dancers with a ten-foot pole. I looked around as we were driving: McDonald's, Taco Bell, Exxon, Pizza Hut. No pyramids, no gauzy shapes. But Egypt was there. There was Egypt Photo, for instance, a mysterious photo shop where, I imagined, pictures were obtained by means of a photographic technique known only to the ancient Egyptians. At the college, I gingerly probed the mystery some more. The people of Southern Illinois were known, I was told, either as Egyptians or as Suckers. The mystery was growing. Finally, an eminent historian told me that the appellation "Egypt" may have attached to the region during a crop failure in the 1830s when this area's corn crop survived, thus causing the neighboring counties to look upon it as ancients looked upon the granaries of Egypt. It seemed far-fetched, even given the nineteenth century's well-known penchant for grandeur. The explanation for suckers was even more outré: during a period of drought, the people in the region drank water by means of cane straws from

DAVID GRAHAM: *Football Players*
(COURTESY OF THE PHOTOGRAPHER)

crayfish holes in the ground. The mythic origin of these Egyptian suckers continued to baffle me until a shady guy with sunglasses, who used to be a professor until they denied him tenure, pulled me aside and whispered: "Little Egypt was a belly dancer famous for her performances at the 1893 Columbian Exposition in Chicago." Aha! This famous hootchy-kootchy gal was right from around here. And it is she who taught the locals how to suck from crayfish holes with cane straws. It figures, doesn't it?

SANDRA RUSSELL CLARK: *The Gotham Times*
(COURTESY OF THE PHOTOGRAPHER)

The East

Those who live near the sea, feed more on fish than on flesh, and often encounter that boisterous element. This renders them more bold and enterprising; this leads them to neglect the confined occupations of the land. They see and converse with a variety of people; their intercourse with mankind becomes extensive.

—J. Hector St. John de Crévecoeur,
Letters from an American Farmer, 1782

He is a tall man with square shoulders . . . But his color is pale and he seems soiled . . . he looks dazed as if he were not part of the world in which he is walking, as if life had come suddenly under a shadow which he could see no way of getting out of and had no means of accounting for. You can't tell whether he is a skilled mechanic or a former auto dealer or a bank cashier or a department store manager . . . But he wanders incongruously along West Fifty-eight Street past the restaurants with smart French names and the half-empty apartment houses where liveried doormen guard the doors.

—Edmund Wilson, "A Man in the Street," 1932

For my sins I live in the city of New York.

—Ted Berrigan, "Whitman in Black"

The East Coast is, for me, composed of equal parts of nostalgia and ongoing concern. I lived in both Baltimore and New York. I have nostalgia for both, but mostly for Baltimore where I will never return to live again. New York is a palimpsest and it always looms as a future possibility. Other places, such as Boston or Philadelphia, are perennial stops in this voyaging life of mine. I love their foods and their waterfronts, I have friends there. I can write about these places, but it is hard to generalize about such multifaceted, intimate places. I have navigated a multitude of communities, accents, and architectures in this region. The following are mere glimpses.

Boston

In february 1974 or thereabouts
in one of those years when none
of my friends had jobs,
a friend with a job being such a rarity
we respected him like an elder
and pitied him like one—
in the coldest month of such a year
my friend Janosz Batki got a job
& not just a job but a job with
an impressive title at Harvard University
a title so impressive it was twice hyphenated
and I admired him immensely
but mostly envied & hated him for it
because it seemed to me that Janosz
who had done little in his life except
go to that horrid Iowa Workshop
write a few poems
and translate the complete poetic works
of the great Hungarian poet Attilla Joszef

was less deserving than I who though young
and innocent of the snakepits of academia
had the aura of greatness about me
and deserved all the jobs—
anyway in one of those years in the horrid
month of february when I was living in New York City
and dreaming of Italy,
I took the train to Boston to visit Janosz
and imagined him ensconced in a splendid
Victorian room with a blazing fireplace,
silent servants serving amber spirits
to the faithful young arrayed at his feet
and the closer I got to these regions
the brighter the fire the more amber the liquid
the more resplendent the scantily clad youth
upturned in admiration—and by Rhode Island
where Ted Berrigan was born
I almost turned back unable to suffer the miseries
of my jealous imagination—
Janosz did live in a splendid manse
but in the mansard of that manse
and the fireplace was a tiny space heater
that threw barely enough heat to warm the feet
of my friend shivering with a cold under a tattered blanket
because he couldn't afford the heat on what Harvard paid him
for his double-hyphenated job.
He was happy to see me
because he thought I had enough money to take him out for a
hot meal
which I later did
but then it was too cold to go out—

a blizzard had started up and the snow
was burying the house—
we took some psylocybin instead—
and Stratis Haviaras joined us—
he is now poetry librarian at Harvard
but I think back then he was a jobless Greek
poet and novelist-in-the-making
certainly he didn't look to me like he had a job:
the humiliation of two employed poets would have killed me—
and when the psylocybin came on it wasn't so cold anymore—
we did drink from a jug of red wine
and wrestled some very peculiar shadows
typical it seemed to me of New England and Harvard
some type of anguished emersonian maxims
with a touch of dickensonian melancholy
like a drum and a violin
and in fact we played some sort of musical instruments
until dawn
when we went out into the fresh snow and had coffee
in Harvard Square and I admired through sleepy lids
the brightness of all that sportive yet pensive youth
that was Janosz's good luck to pervert
even though Harvard didn't pay him enough for the heat—
and that was the first time I was in Boston.

The second time
I was given a personal tour by the poet John Weiners
who in looking for a certain liquor store
made me stand at certain undistinguished street corners
and said:
"This is where Charles Olson first told me he liked my poetry,"

and, "This is where Bob Creeley hugged me,"
and I remember those places well because I stared hard
there were some buildings there with steps
and a little grocery store on the corner—
and I really liked that tour & have adopted it.
Now when I show people around I take them only to such
points of personal interest
and point out to them the significant encounters
which somehow never seem to happen in front of well-known
landmarks

& if they do, the monuments overshadow the moments
& take credit for them when their role is simply to mark the spot,
to provide lovers with an easy point of reference.
This is why European lovers have met for centuries under famous
clocks.
Of course one can imagine a johnny appleseed boswell type
following one around ready to plant a tree whenever
a significant moment occurs—
or Johnny Appleseed firm of Philip Johnson, Inc
to raise a supermarket on the spot—
Here where Tacitus peed a Safeway rose.
(Latin, please)
But I was still living in New York then
and while Boston was decidedly exotic because of its monuments
and because of the remarkable hostility that Louisa Solano
the proprietess
of Grolier's bookstore showed me when we first met
but which she subsequently retracted because I must have
entered her list of the Good who did battle with the Bad
many of whom bad and good shared the shelves in her

microcosm of poesy
and while it was true of Boston as it was true of Panonia
or London at this time,
"am none the wiser, none the better for it, the pay is too high,"
(Latin, please)
I was beginning to acquire a sneaky fondness
for its consistent deflation of my sentiments—

It was the third time I came to Boston
—I was living in California then—
that things took a truly strange turn.

Jack Powers, I believe, though I could be wrong
—if I am please correct me promptly—
on behalf of the ex–mental patients' league
invited me to provide an evening of poetic entertainment
to the gentlemen of the halfway house he lived in.
It was once again winter
which seemed to be my Bostonian season
but not furious winter this time
but one of those ice wind in-between times
when a mean gray sky takes large bites of the citizens
with total impunity and not much response
and I stood before the ex-mental gentlemen
trying out some long poems which I had conceived
in another clime and under considerably bluer skies
& as I unfolded my complicated insights
a kind of wind began in the room
caused by the rocking back and forth in their chairs
of nearly one hundred human beings
who had picked up the thread of my thoughts

and adjusted it to their own internal rhythms
& I found myself likewise rocking back & forth on the balls of
my feet
which caused them to rock faster
causing me to rock faster
until the lengthy verses conceived in the leisure of my nude
beach
in paradise
began resembling some motors out of whack
racing to the finish line at Daytona—
it was exhausting.
Following the strenuous labor
we commended ourselves to a bar around the corner
where the entourage began to drink my modest fee
& that was alright
until the bar closed
& I found myself conversing with a barefoot couple
the female side of which was emitting steady but poignant
electrical shocks to my alcohol-altered person
though in all fairness she would have emitted them
under any circumstances
while the longhaired man who accompanied her
seemed like a benign animal of indistinct sexuality
with whom it was unnecessary to do battle
since he signalled no proprietary values at all
& I had no idea who these people were
even though they told me that they were some of the Walkers
a group of young idealists who had decided to walk from
San Francisco to Moscow in order to bring about World Peace
& they had already walked from San Francisco to Boston—
hundreds of them—though only a few had made it

the rest having found World Peace too great a pedestrian
undertaking—
but these two were among the stubborn ones
& they invited me to spend what remained of the night
at the communal house in West Medford
where the rest of the heroes could be found—
Drawn by the electrical current of the female walker
we arrived at a modest wooden house in West Medford
a tiny dwelling entirely filled from kitchen floor and attic
with sleeping bodies though some were awake and drinking Mu
tea
in the kitchen with their feet planted on their sleeping
companions
& when I asked where I might bed down
someone made a generous gesture that included the whole house.
The object of my desire having disappeared
I decided to search for her through the darkened rooms,
an undertaking made difficult by the gingerly dance
I had to perform between bodies sprawled in darkness
a not all too graceful dance either given the fact that I was
drunk—
and at long last in a small room that could once have served
as a pantry
I thought I saw her lying there on her back the nipples
that pierced her T-shirt rising and falling in the rhythm of sleep
& the arm of a strong rather large man was draped proprietarily
under her head—but no matter—I had come this far.
I dislodged a number of sleepers and threw myself at her side
whereby followed a long & timeless choreography
which saw the infinitesimal motions of our bodies
grow increasingly agitated until I held her naked in my arms

& was inside her without the man's arm having moved—
an excruciatingly delightful situation given that our lovemaking
was nearly without motion & came to a complete stop
every time his controlling limb or his body appeared to wake.
The gray light of the West Medford dawn found me sleepless
& aroused & unreleased as I rose to make my way back to
California.
In order to get there I had to hitchhike to Logan Airport
which is what I did. A car stopped. In it was a man
who asked me what kind of accent was it that came thickly
from my swollen lips
and after I told him Romania
he appraised me silently for a few moments
and asked: "Would you like
to go back to your native country?"
Right now, I replied, I would like to get back to my bed
in California.
But tomorrow, he insisted, would you like
to parachute back to your own country?
It can be arranged.
He worked for an organization, he confessed,
that could and did parachute former nationals back
behind the Iron Curtain
where they earned a hefty paycheck for blowing up bridges.
I will consider it, I said,
but you must take me all the way to Logan so I can think about it.
And I slept all the way
parachuting with my anonymous paramour
behind enemy lines until we got to Logan
& I flew off noting that Boston once more

was a place where experiences & weather combine
to react uniquely upon my person.

The next few times I came to Boston
the weather remained constant—
you could carry meat around without any fear
of its spoiling—
and there was another established motif
that was invariable and obvious,
namely the car or rather the idea of car.
One late fall that was of course wintry
I was a guest on "Car Talk" with Arlo Guthrie
& displayed my ignorance of automobiles to millions
of radio listeners who thought I was Yakov Smirnoff—
& another time I talked about cars on a bridge
in the middle of a heavy flow of traffic
in my capacity as commentator for WGBH TV—
and another time I spent three hours in a taxi
stuck on the freeway with a Nigerian cabdriver
who demonstrated to me brilliantly the need
for world revolution
in which I believed wholeheartedly at that moment—
only world revolution could have possibly freed us
from that freeway—or a miracle ordered personally
by the Pope whose attention to traffic in catholic towns
exceeds and supercedes all other concerns—
it's how Rome gets by—
Boston is a kind of Rome. Only colder.

Baltimore

In 1977 I had a moment of sheer existential panic. I was living with my wife, my son, and son-to-come in Monte Rio, California, a paradise for the hopeless where time stood still. We were broke. My pitiful freelancing barely paid the modest mortgage on our shack over the blackberry ravine. There were no jobs to be had anywhere and on top of it our friends started to die all around us in freaky accidents, destroying the little community that until then had made being poor and stupid reasonably tolerable. We sold our house and went to Europe in the vague hope of settling in France or Italy. It was not to be. We spent most of the modest profit from the house sale eating bad food at overpriced restaurants. On the way back from Europe to California we stopped in Baltimore to visit our friend Michelle Neff.

Michelle insisted that we stay for the summer in the basement apartment of a friend on Calvert Street and we did. In fact, we stayed for six incredibly creative years. Baltimore in 1978 was pretty much in the dumps, a blue-collar town singing the recession blues, but compared to California it was a veritable vortex of energy. After ten years on the West Coast I couldn't believe that here was a place where people got up in the morning and *did* things. I started getting up and doing a whole lot of depressing and low-paying things. I started teaching part-time at Essex Community College, CCB downtown, the Poets-in-the-Schools Program. All these jobs might have been bearable if I'd had a car. Instead, I took buses everywhere. I waited for hours in wintry slush on cold days for buses that rarely came. Nonetheless, even this misery had its bright side. My son Tristan was born in 1978 and got well bundled for his ride in the shopping cart to the grocery store. (The shopping cart belonged to the store, but it was our main locomotion for a year, thank you A&P!) I met the local poets who were sweetly encouraging: Rodger Kamenetz, Kraft Rompf, David Hilton, Daniel Mark Epstein, Joe Cardarelli, David Franks, Clarinda Harris Lott, Diane Fancey. Later, when Baltimore's poetic community started thriving, people like Sandie Castle, Tom DiVenti, Chris Toll, and Richard Sober brought incredible energy to what became a true literary renaissance for the town of Poe and Mencken.

The town itself in its pre-Rouse shabby working-class glory was a great source of inspiration. We moved to Melville and Frisby by the old Memorial Stadium. On game nights the street was lit like a stage by the bright stadium lights and everyone sat on their porches listening to the games with the stereo addition of the crowd sounds engulfing us. I was writing my autobiographical book, *In America's Shoes*, according to the dictates of the fans. When they applauded I took a bow as if they were applauding my writing. When they booed I crossed out what I'd just written.

In my spare time I haunted the area between the Peabody Museum, the weed-covered lots by the harbor before Harbor Place and Fells Point. It was all very potent, magical, and nostalgic. The Peabody, the greatest collection of bric-a-brac in America, reminded me of the Bruckenthal Museum in my childhood in Sibiu, Transylvania. There was rarely anybody in it and I communed at leisure with the unicorn horn and the Japanese armor. On Charles Street, just up from the

Peabody, is the house where the American Psychoanalytical Society was founded. I met a brilliant schizophrenic at a little coffee place on the square who gave me a psychic reading of the house up to the floor where Sigmund Freud is said to have stayed. When he got to that floor he became so distressed he ran away screaming. I also used to sit on the steps of the cathedral in that square, on the spot where F. Scott Key collapsed and died. The bums were certainly literate in those days. One dignified street person wearing a threadbare tux jacket told me that he'd been spending every day reading Mencken at the Pratt Library.

In 1979 things started looking up. I got a job teaching writing at Johns Hopkins for a year, thanks to John Barth, whom I met at a party. I took my first graduating Writing Program class to a strip joint on the Block. I also got a hangover from F. Scott Fitzgerald who used to live in an apartment Hopkins uses for visiting writers. I had two beers with a friend of mine there. Next day I had a *gin* hangover, one of Scotty's old ones that'd leapt straight out of the wall into my head.

That same year I began contributing to the Op-Ed page of the *Baltimore Sun*, thanks to the generosity of Stephens Broening, a literate and aristocratic gentleman who had been the paper's Moscow correspondent. I also started writing a column, "Melville & Frisby," for the *City Paper*. The publisher, Mr. Russ Smith, paid me a niggardly thirty-five dollars per piece, a sum negotiated with great difficulty up from twenty-five dollars. In 1981 Margot Hammond became editor of the roto section (now defunct) of the *Sun*. She hired me to write "La Vie Bohème," a weekly column where I indulged my growing love for the city and its many oddballs who sometimes threatened me with bodily harm for writing about them. In 1983, Jo Ann Tubman, a reporter at Baltimore's Public Radio station, asked me to read one of my newspaper pieces on tape. She sent it to Art Silverman at National Public Radio in Washington, and that's how my weekly column on "All Things

Considered" got its start. The same year I started teaching at the University of Baltimore where I began publishing a literary magazine with the help of Lawrence Markert and Chris Toll. This magazine, *Exquisite Corpse*, lasted fourteen years.

Baltimore was growing and changing just as I was. We were growing busier, and more exciting. The Empire Salon, a former beauty shop-turned-bookstore-cum-performance-space on St. Charles Street, became for a brief time the locus of an explosive literary scene. The Empire Salon vanished as abruptly as it had appeared, but the new Baltimore School was there to stay. My own illusory sense of well-being vanished just as abruptly when my employment at the University of Baltimore came to an end. We had to, regretfully, leave the town to go to where the work was. In 1984 we moved to Louisiana.

In retrospect, I miss two places most of all: the Mt. Royal Tavern late in the afternoon drinking lazy beers with local bohemians, and the cul-de-sac on Gordon Road where we lived briefly, a place that was like country right in the heart of the city. Oh, and some other things: Poe's grave in a Halloween snowstorm before they opened it up for tourists, when we had to climb over the spiky fence and feel in imminent danger of impalement. Dangling feet off an old pier at Fells' Point watching boats bobbing there. That, and crab cakes.

New York

C onde Nast Traveler sent a squadron of reporters around the world
to see how helpful the locals might be to the baffled tourist.
Getting lost in a foreign city can sometimes be one of the best things
to happen to you, partly because it is a chance to ask questions and
encounter the natives. But these investigators were after more than
simple encounters: they were out to gauge attitudes, measure rudeness
and courtesy, ascertain cross-cultural habits and, generally, blow the
whistle on commonly accepted myths. For instance, everyone has heard
that the French are snooty to the lost English speaker. Are they? And
who hasn't been weaned on the tale of New Yorkers' razor-sharp wits
and brusqueness?

This last one was my job. Others got to go to Great Britain, France,
Singapore, and Italy, relatively easy posts, where feigning ignorance of
language and locale is no great shakes—since all but the locals *really*
know how to say it and where it is. These easy assignments, which
required only a minimum of acting talent, yielded a variety of results,
alluded to throughout this report.

But *I* got to go to New York, where I was to pretend to be a lost
foreign tourist trying to find some of New York's better known attrac-

tions. That, you will agree, requires the stamina of an athlete, the acting ability of a De Niro, and the sense of irony of Dada meister Tristan Tzara.

Of course, I *am* a foreigner. I speak with an accent that varies in thickness depending on how self-conscious I feel. But I am no tourist, having once lived in the Big Apple for two years. And I come back every three months or so. I have acquaintances who don't even know that I don't live in New York anymore. I run into them, and they blandly say, "How are you?" as if I'd just moved out to another neighborhood. It's inconceivable to them that anybody might leave New York. New York is a universe: true New Yorkers might suspect the existence of other places, but they do not quite believe in them. Many New Yorkers still see the world like the famous Saul Steinberg map of the United States on which only New York and Los Angeles are clearly marked. There is nothing in between. This sort of thinking may suggest arrogance, but in fact the residents of this great city are extreme provincials. They live in their own neighborhoods with the dedication of peasants to their villages. When I lived here I lived in Greenwich Village. I had little reason, beyond business, to go above Fourteenth Street. Going to midtown or uptown was an expedition, like going to a different country. I took supplies. Wore different clothes.

Whenever I return to New York, I feel immediately at home. I resume my wanderings where I left off last time. I take my place at my favorite café, I frequent the same restaurants, I enter the same shops, I buy my paper at the same corner, and I take mental inventory of establishments and landmarks to make sure that nothing has changed. I feel quite proprietary about the place, as a matter of fact. Maybe those acquaintances are right: once a New Yorker, always a New Yorker. Maybe the Big-in-between *doesn't* really exist. After a few days here I begin to doubt.

As for the rudeness of New Yorkers, I had my own theories, prior to this assignment. One time, I came back to New York after a few months in Baltimore. I hailed a cab and I had barely opened the door when the cabbie shouted, "Close the door already!" Now, it didn't seem to me that I'd been terribly slow. When I got in, he asked me: "Where are you from?" I said: "Baltimore." "They wear shoes there?" he shot back. That was funny. Maybe it was rude, too. I don't know. If it makes you laugh, it's probably just funny. If it's rude, it ought to make you angry.

New York is fast. In certain circumstances, this could pass for rudeness. When people are in a hurry, they dispense with formalities. Now, to Europeans and to Asians, this is the acme of rudeness. For them, information is only valid if it comes wrapped in a pretty package of pleases, may-I's, and thank yous. In Paris, for instance, should you want to know what time it is, you must ask: "If you please, may I be so rude as to ask you what time does that exceedingly pretty timepiece that you are wearing tell us it is and I thank you in advance for such interruption and assure you of my contrition for this impertinence of which I am solely responsible?" And then you may or may not find out what time it is.

I know this because I returned from Paris scarcely three days before this assignment, and I had plenty of experience *really* being a baffled tourist, no pretense whatsoever. At one point, I circled three times around the market at rue de Buci looking for my hotel. Nobody had the slightest idea where it was, and three people ignored me completely when I asked. Only after I used my best French to compliment an ornately dressed uniformed man on his costume, did I get pointed to the right place. In fact, I was standing right in front of it, and the man was the doorman of the hotel. Yes, Ionesco wasn't French for nothing. And, of course, he was Romanian.

To prepare me for my assignment, *Condé Nast Traveler* commissioned hordes of investigators to various cities on the planet to determine the rudeness levels. The Paris investigator, Cathy Kelley, reported that only a man with a beret and a guy in the Tuileries gallery even bothered to take pains on her behalf. Everyone else just waved her brusquely off or claimed to be from different planets. I concur with her experiences. Parisians don't like helping you find things. You must first humiliate yourself for an hour. It takes a lot of French to humiliate yourself for that long. So, unless you're a French professor on vacation, forget about learning anything on the street.

Anyway, here I was, fresh from Paris, ready to take on New York. My detective work began near my hotel, the Gramercy Park, at Lexington Avenue and Twenty-first Street. Not far away, at the intersection of Broadway and Fifth Avenue, at Twenty-third Street, is one of New York's most spectacular landmarks, the Flatiron Building. Completed in 1902 from plans drawn by D. H. Burnham & Co., it scissors its way at an acute angle into the intersection. It looks like a flatiron, a familiar object in the early part of our century. The thought that the building might leave its moorings and start to iron people and streets flat like shirts and trousers must have amused generations of New Yorkers. This building may in fact be the ancestor of pop art, the predecessor of Claes Oldenburg's huge domestic objects. My favorite representation of this well-loved building is a photograph by Rudy Burckhardt, in which it looks like a clitoris. It's an image that captures all the humor and pathos of the city for me. I love to watch this building in the rain when it looks to me more like the prow of a ship than either a flatiron or a clitoris. My publisher, St. Martin's, is located therein, so I'm fond of it in yet another way.

One block from the intersection, on Twenty-third Street and Park Avenue, two fashionably dressed blond women stood just inside the doorway of an elegant shoe store. Armed with a faded postcard of the Flatiron Building, I stepped boldly between them.

"If you forgive me," I said, "do you know where this is?"

I extended the postcard furtively as if it were a dirty picture. I half-expected to hear: "Police! Get this pervert with the postcard!"

Instead, they both studied it, and released a simultaneous sigh of recognition. One of them took my arm and walked me out of the store. She pointed in the direction of the building, holding my arm all the while. It was an extraordinarily friendly gesture.

"Where are you from?" I asked.

"Kiev," she said, in a thick Russian accent, "and my friend is from Leningrad. We love that building!"

After thanking her profusely, I headed for the small park directly opposite the building. Three teenagers, two boys and a girl, in cutoffs, with enormous T-shirts on, were passing a cigarette on a bench. Eager to test them, I slid up with the postcard in my hand. I held it out of sight for a long second until I had their attention, then I tapped on it and said in very bad English: "What you do with this building?"

"We didn't do anything with it," one of them answered in correct but accented English. "It's right behind you!"

He turned and I turned with him and, lo and behold, there it was! Slicing the sky and coming toward us.

"Where are you from?" I asked them.

"Sweden," he said.

So far so good. Here I was, a fake foreigner (though once real) getting good help from real foreigners. Not a native in the bunch. I remembered the last time I'd been in New York. A cabbie, with whom I had a pleasant conversation, said to me when I got out: "When you get back home, tell them you met the last English-speaking cabbie in New York!"

Was it true? Farther up Twenty-third Street, a row of people in wheelchairs were sunning themselves in front of the United Cerebral Palsy offices. Standing behind one of them was a nurse in a starched white uniform with kindly ebony glasses on her face. I presented my postcard so that both she and her charges could study it, and said: "I am new in New York. I love houses. Know you where this house is?"

In an accent as thick as mine but in much better syntax the nurse answered crisply: "That is the Flatiron Building. Twenty-one stories. Up two blocks. You cannot miss it."

"Germany," she said, when I asked.

That was three out of three. My job had now become a quest. I had to find a native New Yorker. If they still existed. The next five attempts were failures. A bakery turned out to be a patisserie and the owner was Algerian. The two employees of a health-food shop were, respectively, Chinese and French. A street vendor of protective whistles was Haitian. They all knew where the Flatiron Building was.

In front of Baruch College on Twenty-first Street near Lexington, students with textbooks sat on benches. A young man with long hair and a small goatee, who looked like a baby beatnik, sprawled on one of the stone benches, gazing insolently at female forms.

"*Parlez vous Français?*" I asked him.

"No," he growled.

My heart beat faster. I thought I had one.

I presented the postcard. "You from New York? You know this house?"

"Yeah," he said, "I haven't the faintest."

There it was. Unmistakably New York, the accent of the baby beatnik spilled harshly forth. He was a native. And he had no idea where the Flatiron Building was.

Pleased with myself, I took a cab downtown to Wall Street. The Flatiron Building is a remarkable landmark, but it is rather obscure. Wall Street, on the other hand, is known the world over. It is shorthand for New York and, often, for America. People who hate us say we are "slaves of Wall Street." Even people in remote tropical jungles know that the price of coconuts has something to do with Wall Street.

I had barely gained the sidewalk when a tall girl in a light calico summer dress came up to me. "Do you know where Wall Street is?" she asked me, in British-accented English.

Now, you have to appreciate this. Here I was, as determined a fake foreigner as ever pounded the sidewalks for *Condé Nast Traveler*, and I had just been challenged at my own game. The truth was that, funny as this encounter was, I really didn't know where Wall Street was. The cab had left me two blocks away on Broad Street because of the traffic. I didn't know the direction. It felt funny to be on the other side.

The way I saw it, I had two choices. I could tell her that I didn't know, or I could lie. Lying, strange as it might seem, is an attractive option in such a case. Years ago, I was in Rome at the time when the Italian premier Aldo Moro was assassinated. There was great confusion. Police sirens were heard everywhere, and official vehicles started tearing down the streets at terrifying speeds. A truck full of *carabinieri* in full regalia, with machine guns, screeched to a halt in front of me. I was wearing a baseball cap, a camera, and a T-shirt that said SURF. One of the soldiers saluted and asked me in Italian, "Where is the Central Police Station?" Mustering all the Italian I knew, I pointed in several directions at once and directed him. He thanked me and they took off that way. I felt most gratified by my action. I was no longer a tourist. I became a citizen of Rome that day.

Jonathan Border, the Condé Nast investigator in Rome, reported that he received a great deal of help there. People bent over maps, gave complex directions, and seemed to be generally accurate after acknowledging the difficulty of getting around the labyrinthine streets of the ancient metropolis. One man, instead of trying to explain, offered him a ride on his motor scooter. I believe that Mr. Border was lucky. When I visited Rome, I was given so many wrong directions, I concluded that Romans were perverse. That was partly the reason why I myself misled the *carabinieri*. The other reason was that I really enjoyed doing it.

Anyway, here I stood before my mirror in the real world, an English girl trying to find Wall Street. I tried a third approach.

"I'm not exactly sure where it is," I said, "but I'm looking for it myself. Why don't we both ask someone else?"

We approached a Chinese man selling watches on the sidewalk. The watches were displayed on top of a cardboard box covered with pages from the day's edition of the *Wall Street Journal*. Just to reinforce the correctness of our choice, the headline of an article partly obscured by a fake Rolex read, "Chinese Exchange Heats Up on News of Pacific-Asia Pact."

But, despite all the right signs, the approach was not successful. The man said, "Why go there? These watches better!" He had mistaken Wall Street, it seemed, for a rival watch dealer.

The Condé Nast agent in Singapore reported that the success rate for obtaining information there is only fifty percent. Curtness accompanied the language barrier. Only a teenage Chinese girl who was taking English in school and some university students gave proper directions.

After two more unsuccessful attempts, involving one obvious tourist and a deli-counter server in the midst of a to-go order for one dozen pastrami sandwiches on rye with Russian dressing and coleslaw, we found Wall Street ourselves. In the depths of the thronged canyon, my English friend and I avoided swinging briefcases and parted. She wanted to visit the exchange to see for herself the throbbing flow of America's business blood. I had already seen the exciting spectacle, so I took my leave. And continued my quest.

Ever since the man with the watches, the thought had been gnaw-
ing at me that I should ask more street peddlers in the environs where
Wall Street was. The juxtaposition of small business and big business
appealed to me somehow.

In a small park halfway between Wall Street and the World Trade
Center I espied a row of small-time merchants peddling everything
from high-fashion scarves to engraved Zippo lighters and the ever-
ubiquitous watches. I began with the Zippo man.

"Wall Street?" he said, in highly inflected Jamaican English, "Man,
what do I have to do with that Wall Street? I have my own business,
don't you see!"

A couple of the fellows laughed. But they were friendly, so instead
of directions, I was treated to a sociopolitical analysis of peddling,
money, capitalism, America, and life in general. The consensus, as far
as I could tell, was that America is still the land of opportunities if you
have the money, but it's impossible to get the money if nobody buys
anything and all they want is directions . . . to Wall Street. I got the
message and bought a scarf. It was cheap, considering the plentiful free
advice.

My final query as to the whereabouts of America's financial heart
was addressed to two long-legged, longhaired Latin beauties waiting for
a bus on Rector Street.

"We don't know!" one of them answered curtly, with the air of
someone who was waiting for a bus and who was, moreover, suspicious
of the question as if it had a hidden agenda. I suppose that when one
is a long-legged, longhaired Latin beauty wearing short shorts, questions
from strangers might well have a hidden agenda. I chalked this temporary setback to the situation, not to rudeness and locale.

Later, I had a double espresso at an outdoor café near Columbus
Circle, and tried to summarize my experience. New Yorkers, I decided,

are all helpful, friendly, enterprising, and haven't been here very long. Native New Yorkers, if they still exist, may or may not live up to the myth of rudeness. What is certain is that the new New Yorkers I had met knew more about the city than the rare natives.

When I lifted my eyes from my thoughtful espresso I saw that I was standing next to the Vegetarian Heaven Restaurant, a Chinese-Jewish establishment that specializes in fake real dishes, such as pork dumplings, which are really skillful forgeries made out of soy. My muse was really laying it on thick. And she wasn't about to stop.

Across the street, two Italian boys were drawing a bare-breasted Madonna with colored chalk on the pavement. A tin cup on the ground bore the sign: THIS IS HOW WE MAKE OUR LIVING. ASK US QUESTIONS! BE GENEROUS!

What else can I say? I rose, crossed over, dropped a dollar in the cup, and asked: "Do you know how to get to Lincoln Center?"

"Practice, practice," one of them said, and broke into delighted laughter.

"That's Carnegie Hall!" I huffed.

Ha-ha.

DAVID GRAHAM: *Bridge*
(COURTESY OF THE PHOTOGRAPHER)

E P I L O G U E

I can imagine
having written another book
had I been someone else
a cyclist or a pedestrian
taking two years to go from city to city
or one of those intrepid souls
who re-created the Mormon trail.
Had I been a scholar
I might have brought forth
the facts of buildings and people
in a manner guaranteed to teach
something I haven't yet learned.
The speed of my journeys
by jet and by car
knew neither direction nor geography
so I gave geography and direction
to my cities while being there
and to my book while writing it
knowing only too well
the provisional nature
of space in our time
and the tricks of a writer
trying to order what was only chance after all.
Dear Reader, forgive my trivial
impressions of your worlds
I was there but a moment.
There was love in it.

ANDREI CODRESCU has been in nearly perpetual motion ever since leaving his native Sibiu, Romania, in the mid-sixties. His voluntary and involuntary exile has spanned four decades. Some of his travels were documented in the Peabody–winning movie, *Road Scholar*, and in the book of the same name. Among his many collections of essays are *The Muse Is Always Half-Dressed in New Orleans*, *The Dog with the Chip in His Neck*, and *Zombification*, all published in hardcover by St. Martin's Press and in paperback by Picador USA. He is the author of two novels, *The Blood Countess* and *Messiah*, and the founder of *Exquisite Corpse: A Journal of Letters & Life*. He lives in New Orleans and commutes by Greyhound to teach writing at LSU in Baton Rouge.